Smt Renuka Chowdhury *MP, Rajya Sabha and former Union minister of State for Ministry of Women and Child Development, Government of India* releasing **"Janani—Mothers, Daughters, Motherhood"** *in presence of* **Ms Rinki Bhattacharya,** *author. Also seen in the picture:* **Prof Rama Baru,** *Centre of Social Medicine and Community Health, JNU,* **Ms Urvashi Butalia,** *feminist writer and Publisher,* **Dr Zarina Bhatty,** *former President, Indian Association of Women's Studies and* **Ms Chitra Mudgal,** *Renowned Writer, Novelist and Social Activist.*

Release of **"Janani— Mothers, Daughters, Motherhood"** at an even held in starmark, Kolkata.

Business India

11 February 2007

Love, pain and anger

Motherhood is one of the fundamental tenets of Indian womanhood. Patriarchal ideology sees it as the manifestation of "stri dharma" or woman's duty and transforms her either into a self-sacrificing goddess, or rejects her for infertility. *Janani*, edited by Rinki Bhattacharya, propels us into an emotionally charged world of mother-daughter experiential encounters.

Nearly 12 years in the making, this anthology of 19 autobiographical voices coming from diverse fields, was a "spontaneous response", states Bhattacharya, to the maternal experience of the "empty nest" syndrome, when "children, like birds, have flown away". Shashi Deshpande, Kamla Das, Mallika Sarabhai, Urmilla Pawar, Nabaneeta Dev Sen, Neela Bhagwat, C.S. Lakshmi, Deepa Gahlot, Anwesha Arya are to name a few whose straight from the heart articulations have enriched this collection. The text has a forward by well-known academic and scholar Jashodhara Bagchi, which sets in context the tenor of the collection by recapitulating some of the motherhood debates thrown up by the 1970s' second wave of the Women's Movement in the West.

Janani has been divided in three sections, "Our Mothers", "Ourselves" and "Our Children". The exploration of the dual relationship is fraught with a gamut of emotions ranging from love, pain, anger

and gentle humour. Dalit writer Urmilla Pawar's widowed mother sees motherhood as "a cross the woman carries", likening it to "committing *Sati*". When commiserated for her awful fate of being left with three daughters, the mother's grieving voice pronounced: "All children are equal in a

JANANI: MOTHERS, DAUGHTERS, MOTHERHOOD
Edited by: Rinki Bhattacharya
Published by: SAGE Publications
Price: Rs 280
Pages: 200

mother's eyes". "No I did not love her, but I was proud of her," states Bharati Roy, the emotional restraint giving way after her mother's death, as she acknowledges her love and psychological dependence on her. Ray's mother, a gold medalist and a 1930s graduate of Delhi's Indraprastha College, became a Hindu *pativrata*, neglecting herself. The point of bonding occurs in the last phase of the mother's illness as she admits that her greatest mistake had been. "I have not done my duty to myself." C.S. Lakshmi's mother, in a vegetarian household, cooked eggs for her children, saying it was doctor's advice.

Alamelu too subverted rules while seeming to comply. You don't have to be a biological mother to experience the "magical bond of motherhood" believes Dhiruben Patel, on whom motherhood was thrust.

Nabaneeta Dev Sen's upbringing of two daughters as a single parent aided by a supportive mother, presents a touching and humorous picture of three generational interaction. Shashi Deshpande states "selflessness and creativity are uneasy partners" and concludes, "to be a mother does not rule out everything else in life. I'm a human being first, a mother next." The experiences of an adoptive mother, another woman's determination not to fall into" the minefield of parenthood" and the confession piece "The Mother Who Wasn't", by a woman who had to terminate her pregnancy in her teens and years later, experienced, as a young married woman, the trauma of carrying her child full term only to give birth to a still born daughter, brings alive the multiple shapes of motherhood.

Janani is undoubtedly a valuable asset to Women's Studies. It should, however, be read not just by women but men too – by fathers who perhaps need to ponder on what after all makes motherhood different from fatherhood?

Krishna Sarbadhikary

---

marie claire

November 2006

Motherhood is a cliché, but this complex, multi-layered exploration by writers from different vantage points is a thought-provoking, intelligent and intimate odyssey into worlds that so far have beem little understood.

Janani is a richly rewarding read of the many ways in which mother and daughters view their unique and constantly changing relationship. Most stories have a feminist sub-text. Memories, insights and renditions are all viewed through a woman's gaze. This makes them refreshingly different while binding them to other writing by women as well.

Depending on one's own experiences, some stories will have greater resonance

than others. To this reviewer, the stories that had more narrative and less comment. Such as 'My Mother's Gardens' by Tutun Mukherjee or 'When Alamelu Shrugged' by C.S. Lakshmi, carried greater poignancy. Miatreyi Chatterjee's story 'My Mother, My Daughter' reveals reality as one experiences it in informal chats with close family members rather than on the printed page! The many evocative descriptions of food also bring alive the primeval association between motherhood and food.

Though *Janani* clearly challenges stereotypical images, the conflict between

JANANI
Edited by Rinki Bhattacharya
(Rs 280) SAGE Publications

the need of young children for their mothers, and the need of mothers for time and space for themselves occurs in more than one narrative.

The editing could have re-moved some of the multiple exclamation marks in some narratives, and there are a couple of spelling errors. But all in all, this is a book that is honest and real. A book for anyone who is interested in human relationships.

By Gitanjali Prasad

REVIEWS | Celebrating mothers

Reviewed by Sumera S. Naqvi

THOUGH no woman would consciously deny the divine status she receives on becoming a mother, popular debate in the West today questions the very essence related to the pros and cons of motherhood. Is motherhood a blessing or a curse? Reasons for the latter are plenty. Not only has sacred motherhood been misused to bolster the patriarchal systems that have for decades flourished in feudal societies, it is an extra burden today for working families trying to make ends meet in capitalist societies. Mechanised lifestyles leave suffocating time limits to raise children on a strict schedule. For parenting these days is not just about raising kids but also consciously providing for their proper education, nutrition and general upbringing. Is motherhood then, a celebrated, fulfilling experience or an adieu to a hassle-free life of freedom?

Having thrown into one fold, poignant accounts of Indian daughters paying "belated homage to their mothers" including single, step and so on, editor Rinki Bhattacharya has reflected through Janani, that the idea of motherhood is still ravishing and idealistically cherished despite the stark industrialised realities clamped on it. "Why do human beings need a motherly figure throughout their life while, on comparison, animals forget their mothers the moment they become self-reliant?" asks Dhiruben Patel, contributor of the essay 'Motherhood and me' in the book. Patel has experienced motherhood not by actually being a mother but by hoping to be one. Though most of us take our mothers for granted for being there and providing us with unconditional love, the world is full of half-animals who forget their parents once they find their own legs to stand on solid ground — a hapless child wouldn't think of a life without a mother.

Though women in the West have been chanting slogans for a reformation in the institutionalisation of motherhood for a long time now, movements supporting them still have a long way to go. Due to longer academic years and challenging career options taken up by women, marriages are delayed, fertility ages of women altered and motherhood experienced late in life. It was reported in the press recently that the biological clocks of Italian women now tick longer — reaching 29-30 years from 25, while in Germany, the rate of population growth has drastically fallen because many women shy away from raising families. "I would rather be single than too-muchsome!" said a 40-year-old German friend when asked why she hadn't tied the knot.

The late sociologist Jesse Bernard had

jotted some significant points in her book a long time back in recognition of the mother who "fight[s] those aspects of society that make childbearing and child rearing stressful rather than fulfilling experiences". She believed that at the turn of the 21st century, women's movements will have gained an effective base to establish that a woman can be more than just a mother. Too bad, at the turn of the century, issues like maternal leaves for working mothers, dependable social support systems, flexible workplaces, part-time and better opportunities for professional advancement are still insurmountable

Such a litany of issues also resemble the life of a typical working mother in the east, though the environment in which she brings up children is a tad different. She is part of the new brand of women who succeeded the stay-in mothers of yore, who devoted their lives to the kitchen and the bellies of their family. These stay-in mothers may have been fairly educated but they stayed back at home to look after their families which included in-laws, children and husbands. In Janani, many daughters have narrated how their mothers were married young and studied after their marriage, not to foster ambitions but for personal enrichment.

A daughter reminisces her mother being very fond of studying but having to curtail it because of her early marriage. Yet another remembers that her mother played a musical instrument very well but she could not pursue her passion with due attention. Though none of the daughters complain of a depressing patriarchal environment in the backdrop of the lives of their compassionate mothers, a die-hard feminist bosoming western overtures may dismiss such sugary narratives for being a hoax into women's enslavement.

Why have the daughters not felt such an injustice against their mothers in the name of absolute motherhood? Perhaps such a premise is food for another book, for she confesses, Janani is a collection of accounts by women who were not "merely mothers. Nor were we those eternally sobbing, sacrificing stereotypes of mothers thrown up routinely on the Bollywood screen!" The contributors are working mothers who, unlike their mothers who took pains at administering every minute detail of devoted motherhood, are "eminent writers, performing artists, activists and feminist scholars". One moving account is by Maithili Rao, a film critic based in Mumbai, who narrates her mother's courageous ordeal, who was married at the age of 17 to a man who was already married and had three children, "the oldest being just seven years younger than her," and showered them with so much love. While another story by Dhiruben Patel, an accredited writer in India, who had no children but felt the pangs of motherhood for the children brought to her tutelage.

These accounts are not a gripe to nature. They are a celebration of motherhood, a reminder of the fact that though mothers in the coming years may face a different set of issues caused by the 'seismic shifts' that reshape cultures and societies in various time periods, a mother's caress will always render cushiony comfort to her child.

THE HINDU
METROPLUS
Online edition of India's National Newspaper

Thursday, 30 November 2006

By woman borne

**Rinki Bhattacharya has edited a collection of stories on motherhood. Rana Siddiqui speaks to her.
In Bristol, they have a School of Policy Making for such sufferers, something that India needs to have.**

For a person like Rinki Bhattacharya, who grew up in a household frequented by poets, authors and filmmakers, writing, but naturally, comes as a catharsis. The 64-year-old writer, filmmaker, activist and free-lance journalist, and daughter of the famed filmmaker Bimal Roy, Rinki has quite a few book titles to her credit. From penning books on a serious subject domestic violence, as in "Behind Closed Doors: Domestic Violence In India" and "Indelible Imprints, an essay in Uncertain Liaisons", or about her acclaimed father as in "Bimal Roy — A Man of Silence", Rinki, married to filmmaker Basu Bhattacharya, also has brought out a number of cookbooks.

Recently, she was in New Delhi for the release of "Janani", a collection of stories edited by her.

"Janani" (The mother) is a heart-rending collection published by Sage. Well-known personalities like Mallika Sarabhai, Dhiruben Patel, Urmila Pawar, Maitreyi Chatterji and others have contributed to the book. Grouped under three sections — "Our Mothers", "Ourselves" and "Our Children", the stories talk of all aspects of motherhood, including what it means to be neglected by one's grown-up children; living widowed and alone; and how daughters view their mother's ordeal.

Says Rinki about the stories in "Janani", "I had no problem in collecting them because I had almost a dozen of them in my stock, which were a result of my meeting several

TIRELESS CRUSADER Activist Rinki Bhattacharya

writers across the country. And also when I broached the idea, they only welcomed it, because they had been living with the idea for ages. The book has proved to be a catharsis for all, including me."

No volunteers

Being associated with several movements that help the cause of women, especially those working against domestic violence, Rinki has just slowed down on practical demonstrations and devoted herself to building her library of stories that she has had collected during several such interactions with victims. She has a reason for this. "I was running an NGO

for the cause of women in Mumbai but I had to fold it up. There were no young committed volunteers willing to join for it had little money. Those who were running it with me got burnt out because of age, financial crunch, space paucity and lack of trained staff. But I am still associated with Awaaz-e-Niswan, a Mumbai-based NGO run by Shahnaz Sheikh who challenged the concept of triple *talaq*. She is also completely burnt out for the same reason. But whenever they need me for any demonstration, etc., I go there."

Not only that, Rinki is as dedicated to her 12-year-old Bimal Roy Foundation that keeps the legendary filmmaker alive in the hearts "of the government and people" by organising programmes in India and abroad. For four years now the Foundation has been felicitating film personalities we seem to have forgotten. "We were the first to honour Waheeda Rahman and Surraiya and last year we felicitated Nimmi," she informs.

The book has also been launched in the U.K. where Sage has a chapter. Rinki says that even the U.K readers will identify with it because domestic violence is a universal truth. "In Bristol, they have a School of Policy Making for such sufferers, something that India needs to have. Though people like Ila Ben Bhatt and Meera Jaisingh have been doing it in their own way, yet we need to sensitise young people to take up the cudgels," she concludes.

I love you mom, but ...

A recently published anthology of autobiographical writings explores the mut of the relationship between mothers and daughters. **Yasmin Taj** speaks to editor Rinki Bhattacharya on the making of the book.

One doesn't normally draw on the teachings of Rajneesh while referring to a relationship between a mother d her offspring. But the new-age Guru a forgotten age t it well. "The oment a child is rn, the mother is so born. She never sted before. The oman existed, but e mother, never. A ther is something solutely new," he d.

makes sense, pecially when put the context of that ecial relationship ween a mother and r daughter. When u are five, she's ur goddess — you ear your face with lipstick and totter und in her high heels. That's the way it until you are about 13, when she suddenly comes the most ignorant, benighted, -of-touch creature on this planet. And n, somewhere between your twenties thirties, if you are lucky, she becomes ur friend again. And continues to be one he very end.

ki Bhattacharya, director of the Bimal y Memorial Committee — the film ker was her father — showcases the ationship in a book published by Sage ently. Bhattacharya is the editor of ani — Mothers, Daughters, Motherhood, collection which brings together obiographical writings of women from erent walks of life — noted authors, stes, academics — who share their erience of being a mother, a daughter, or . The anthology was recently launched Mumbai and Delhi.

Bhattacharya, the idea of bringing ether the chronicles of these women their experiences as mothers and ghters came about quite suddenly. "This something I had not actually thought ut. I am an art critic and I've always erved that most eminent painters have dealt with mother-daughter relationships in their paintings. Also, I had made a five-minute audio-visual capsule called Janani, or mother as the inventor of life, which won a lot of acclaim. I believe that was the germination of the idea of doing this narrative collection," she says.

The contributors to the book include Kamala Das, Shashi Deshpande, Deepa Gahlot, Mallika Sarabhai,

Woman tales: Rinki Bhattacharya (left) and Union minister Renuka Chowdhury at the launch of Janani

Bharati Roy and Nabaneeta Dev Sen. There is also Urmila Pawar, a Dalit writer, and Bhattacharya's daughter, Anvesha Arya. "Each woman here has her own distinct story to tell and I gave them the space to write it the way they wanted to."

Motherhood, most believe, is a phenomenon that is difficult to define. "That is why this book has a vast spectrum. Many questions are asked and many experiences shared," says Bhattacharya, who has also shot a documentary film called Char Diwari on domestic violence. "I do believe that every woman is thinking through her mother. Our mothers are our reference points."

The collection includes true stories on adoptive motherhood, step-mothering, and single motherhood. On the one hand, the reader encounters the gut-wrenching description of an avoidable abortion, and on the other, the firm choice made by a woman never to be a mother. The narratives vividly depict the whole gamut of the experience of motherhood. "Every piece in the book has an element of stark reality."

The opening piece, by Bharati Roy, begins with her mother's death. "Her narration is extremely candid and honest. She actually talks about her mother becoming old and ugly and then dying," says Bhattacharya.

Dev Sen writes of her two daughters and her own writer mother. And how, post menopause, a new daughter walks into her life. There is a piece in Janani by a Naxalite mother and how she brings up her daughter in spite of adverse conditions. All the narratives underline the view that the mother-daughter relationship is the most simple, and the most complex, of all ties.

A daughter is a mother's gender partner, her closest ally in the family confederacy, an extension of herself. A mother is also her daughter's role model and her biological and emotional road map. Between these two women can spring a strong affinity and an equally strong tension.

My own experience of being a mother or with my mother would not be without nuances," says Bhattacharya. "Initially, I was a very docile and obedient daughter. But then, as I grew up, I changed and became a rebel. In fact, my relationship with my Mom was quite troubled. After I eloped, my mother never accepted me back, though my father did."

Bhattacharya, who suffered violence in her marriage with director Basu Bhattacharya till she walked out of it, believes that her mother loved her "in her own way though she felt a little threatened because of my closeness to my father". On the other hand, she says, "I love being a mother and especially a grandmother. But I do firmly believe that mothers and daughters can never be best friends. At some point in time, the mother always tends to get protective and questioning and I think it's but natural for her to be that way," she adds.

Why hasn't she written her own narrative then? "I have not written about myself in Janani since each of these 19 women has said what I would like to say."

Bhattacharya also reveals that she shares a very strong bond with her daughters. "I am a perfectionist and I almost single-handedly brought up my kids. Every mother and child should have the space where they don't feel threatened, where they can talk to each other about every conceivable thing," she says.

'Progressive laws strengthen reformers'

Be it a newspaper article, a book or a documentary — **Rinki Bhattacharya** *has tackled the issue of domestic violence in unnervi detail. In New Delhi recently to celebrate the launch of her latest book,* **Janani: Mothers, Daughters and Motherhood**, *publish by Sage, she spoke to* **Avijit Ghosh** *on the topics closest to her heart:*

What is your book about?

Janani perhaps started 12 years ago when my children had grown up leaving an empty house. It was traumatic. Many mothers face such a situation. My friends were going through a similar phase. We met and shared our situation. This book is about sharing. The narratives are rooted in reality. They are autobiographical.

We get a glimpse of the changing perspective on motherhood. I did not have to coax any of the writers. We all regret not having done enough for our mothers.

You have written extensively on domestic violence. Do you think the latest Act will help improve the condition of Indian women?

The Act is holistic in its vision. It aims at preventing families from becoming dysfunctional. When there's an act of violence, everyone suffers. The victim suffers, the children suffer, even the pets and domestics suffer. This Act addresses the issue and aims to build a healthier family life by discouraging violence. This will boost women's morale. It will be a deterrent to abusive partners and husbands.

The Supreme Court recently held that a woman who marries after divorce is entitled to custodial rights of her child. Another ruling was on joint ownership of house. How do you look at these developments?

These are important steps. When a woman wants to leave a violent partner, her first fear, she will loose the children's custody. This keeps women down; they prefer to suffer in silence. The above decisions offer additior support to women. Let us not forget th famous film stars and pop artistes like T Turner have suffered in abusive relationshi One wonders what their lives would have be if they had the necessary social support. Th would have jumped out and rebuilt their liv Women are a powerhouse of resource they can rebuild lives from nothing. In Inc legal reforms are followed by social refor A progressive law strengthens the hand reformers.

The movies made by your father Bin Roy often had women in path-breaki roles. Do you think the portrayal women in Hindi films has changed the better over the years?

Bollywood thrives on stereotypes a manufactures more stereotypes. A mode looking westernised heroine switches a sari after marriage. She projects accepted traditional look. But the issue i about portrayal alone, it is about the them of films. In Nagesh Kukunoor's Dor, t traditional women from remote villages ma radical decisions. This was such a progress statement.

New Women

The word Janani or mother automatically conjures up images of self-sacrificing stereotypical women, playing provider, nurturer to perfection. This book is an autobiographical account of women from many walks of life – noted authors, artists, academics several mothers and daughter – about their experience of motherhood. Expect the unexpected. There is a wee bit of the idyllic and euphoric aspect of motherhood but it is interspersed generously with brutally blunt experiences of motherhood that exist but are rarely acknowledged or talked about. Shashi Despande's is one such narration and so is Deepa Gahlot's which reiterates the prerogative of every women so remain childless, if she so desires. These authentic, humane and intimate narratives explore the whole gamut of motherhood in nuanced detail. A compelling and heartwarming read.

TITLE: JANANI: MOTHERS, DAUGHTERS, MOTHERHOOD
EDITED BY: RINKI BHATTACHARYA
Price: Rs 280/-
Publisher: SAGE Publications

4 December 2006

Listen To The Ultrasound

By Anita Roy

Janani—Mothers, Daughters, Motherhood
Edited by Rinki Bhattacharya
SAGE
Pages: 197; Rs: 280

Until recently it seemed as though all books about mothers fell into two categories: those that told you 'how to', and those that said why you should not. First-wave feminism characterised motherhood as "the biological curse of femininity". In the battle of the sexes, mothers were the turncoats.

More than any other experience, motherhood is about duality: virtually a definition of the divided self. In *A Life's Work: On Becoming a Mother*, Rachel Cusk writes that "birth is not merely that which divides women from men: it also divides women from themselves, so that a woman's understanding of what it is to exist is profoundly changed..."

Rinki Bhattacharya's collection is in three parts: 'Our Mothers', 'Ourselves' and 'Our Children'. This simple structure has a curious overall effect of seeing the biological clock run backwards. We start with death beds and end up with cradles.

Five of the eight authors in the first section talk about their mothers' death, and the poignant reversal of roles—when the mother becomes the child to the daughter—that precedes it. The sacrifices made by mothers for their children is a double-edged sword whose legacy is not only emancipation but also guilt. Where Bharati Ray rails against it ("She lived like a shadow of my father"), Maitreyi Chatterji celebrates it: "This is not only one daughter's emotional tribute to her mother but to all the mothers who give up their todays to create

better tomorrows for us."

The second section includes essays by those who, like Dhiruben Patel, haven't given birth, but have nevertheless been mothers. She writes, movingly, that "love for a child heightens one's perceptions and understanding to such a level that one acquires a sixth sense and a third eye". Others paint a bleaker picture. In her brilliant essay, Shashi Deshpande rails against the impossible idealisation of Indian motherhood in which "all attributes are squeezed out of her, so that she is shorn of...even humanhood, leaving behind nothing but motherhood".

Deepa Gahlot's is the only essay against motherhood, and I found myself ruing the missed opportunity for a more serious, hard-edged voice to articulate this position. Her characterisation of mothers as "caged birds" who "lack the courage to be free", I found both simplistic and juvenile.

For a book on motherhood, it's ironic that the strongest piece is on its opposite. Anwesha Arya takes her cue from the opening line of Anne Sexton's poem *The Abortion*: "Somebody who should've been born is gone." It is rare enough that silence shrouding 'the Act' is broken; rarer still that the scars it

> **"...All attributes are squeezed out of her, so that she is shorn of...even humanhood, leaving nothing but motherhood."**

leaves are delineated with such unflinching honesty, and in finely-crafted prose.

Bhattacharya points out the lacunae in the book: "None of the authors enter into the grave issue of Indian society's condemnation of women who fail to give birth to children.... Also, the portrait of mothers who burn their young daughters-in-law is absent from this picture gallery." But notwithstanding the gaps, *Janani* is an important first step towards a more politically astute and personally heartfelt portrait of motherhood in all its complexity.

Love you mom …

Autobiographical narratives that explore the unique bond between mothers and daughters

JANANI–Mothers, Daughters, Motherhood
Edited: Rinki Bhattacharya
SAGE
Price: Rs 280
Pages: 197

Sujata Madhok

Dedicated to the umbilical cord that binds mothers and daughters life-long is a collection of twenty essays on motherhood. *Janani* has been lovingly, thoughtfully designed. Its cover is a mother-nad-child painting by K K Hebbar that evokes an Indian mother in a moment of self-reflection. The essays within reflect the same thoughtful, emotional exploration of the experience of motherhood.

Customarily, in India, it is the mother-son relationship that has been the stuff and substance of folklore and fable, literature and popular culture. In that sense, a book on the mother-daughter relationship is a departure, a small rebellion. *Janani* offers a score of authors, artists, academics and journalists the opportunity to explore this unique relationship. They speak in different voices, sometimes as mothers, at other times as daughters and often as both.

Nostalgia lends its aura to so many of the essays, as women lovingly recreate the lost worlds of childhood.

In a thought-provoking foreword, academician Jasodhara Bagchi comments on the paradox that Hinduism links motherhood to a pantheon of goddesses. The mother goddess herself is called Shakti or energy, imputing divine power to motherhood. Yet, notes Bagchi, "motherhood is so far one of the most disempowering of social roles in

traditional or poor families." The woman's unique, magical power to procreate renders her singularly powerless in patriarchal societies.

Nevertheless, many mothers have made spaces within patriarchal structures for themselves and their daughters, rejecting tradition, gifting freedom to their growing girls. Perhaps it is no coincidence that several of the women who wrote these essays have been active in the autonomous women's movement. Their mothers gave them the self-confidence and independence to go forth and challenge the traditional order.

C S Lakshmi's "When Alamelu Shrugged" recalls how at critical moments her mother shrugged off tradition and "gave her daughters wing".

Married at the age of eleven into a traditional south Indian Brahmin family, Alamelu was creative and unconventional in many ways. She turned even cooking into "a mode of communication, assertion and adventure". One of the loveliest sections in this volume is Lakshmi's recollection of her mother's kitchen redolent with the fragrance of jackfruit jam and tender mango pickle, hot ghee and fiery rasam.

In her youth Alamelu learnt to read English from her husband and taught him Tamil. She stopped playing the veena for years because of her husband's disapproval but later she taught it to her daughters. Her excuse for teaching Lakshmi to dance, at a time when it was not considered entirely respectable, was that the doctor had advised dance as exercise since the girl

was skinny!

When Lakshmi's father opposed her goin to college in Chennai, Alamelu took a ba loan against her jewellery, bought a suitca and four brightly coloured saris and put h daughter on the train.

It is mother like these whom the boo celebrates, Marathi dalit writer Urmi Pawar's story about her mother is sta in its depiction of rural poverty. Her moth worked hard to bring up her children aft the early death of her husband, received jolt when the elder son died and anoth when her second son died. Immersed grief, surrounded by disempowering ritua in a traditional society, she somehow fou the courage to embrace her daughters a assert that she was still a mother.

In another section of the work, activ Jyotsna Kamal shares the joys a trials of single mothering her daught Chetana, carrying her to demonstratio and meetings and giving her a singula unconventional childhood. Chetana h bloomed through it all and today is bo friend and daughter.

Like C S Lakshmi, Tutun Mukherj celebrates her mother's creativit Drawing inspiration from Alice Walke emphasis on "the matrilineal legacy creativity that is passed on", Mukherj recalls how her mother expressed hers in intricate needlework and lace and creating mouthwatering delicaci in the kitchen. "For my mother, t kitchen was a microcosm, a plac of power in a patriarchal househo where the woman's control remain uncontested," She says. The kitch garden was an extension of th space where mother grew herbs a leafy vegetables, limes and lemo and berries for chutneys, Mukher also speaks of Naomi Lewinsk concept of the "Motherline" which the "biological, historical/cultural a unconscious feminine legacy that g passed on from mother to daughte granddaughter".

Rinki Bhattacharya's collection bri together many tender memories lac with sharp insights on the unique bo between mothers and daughters. The bo that will stir nostalgia in every reader v chooses to look into her mother's garde

SAGE Classics

Over the years SAGE has published books that can truly be called classics.

SAGE Classics is a carefully selected list that every discerning reader will want to possess, re-read and enjoy for a long time. These are now priced lower than the original, but is the same version published earlier. SAGE's commitment to quality remains unchanged.

Watch out for more titles in this series.

Other SAGE Classics:

Adoption in India: Policies and Experiences
Vinita Bhargava

Behind Closed Doors: Domestic Violence in India
Edited by Rinki Bhattacharya

Kashmir: Roots of Conflict, Paths to Peace
Sumantra Bose

War and Diplomacy in Kashmir, 1947-48
C. Dasgupta

A Space of Her Own: Personal Narratives of Twelve Women
Edited by Leela Gulati and Jasodhara Bagchi

Mentoring: A Practitioner's Guide to Touching Lives
Sunil Unny Guptan

Buddhism in India: Challenging Brahmanism and Caste
Gail Omvedt

Operation Black Thunder: An Eyewitness Account of Terrorism in Punjab
Sarab Jit Singh

Janani—Mothers, Daughters, Motherhood

❦❧

Janani—Mothers, Daughters, Motherhood

❧❧

edited by
Rinki Bhattacharya

⑤SAGE www.sagepublications.com
Los Angeles • London • New Delhi • Singapore • Washington DC

First published in 2006
This edition published in 2013 by

SAGE Publications India Pvt Ltd
B1/I-1 Mohan Cooperative Industrial Area
Mathura Road, New Delhi 110 044, India
www.sagepub.in

SAGE Publications Inc
2455 Teller Road
Thousand Oaks, California 91320, USA

SAGE Publications Ltd
1 Oliver's Yard, 55 City Road
London EC1Y 1SP, United Kingdom

SAGE Publications Asia-Pacific Pte Ltd
33 Pekin Street
#02-01 Far East Square
Singapore 048763

Published by Vivek Mehra for SAGE Publications India Pvt Ltd, Typeset in 10/12 pt Baskerville by Star Compugraphics, New Delhi and printed at De-Unique, New Delhi.

Library of Congress Cataloging-in-Publication Data

Janani: mothers, daughters, motherhood/edited by Rinki Bhattacharya.
    p. cm.
1. Mothers—India. 2. Motherhood—India. I. Bhattacharya, Rinki.

HQ759. J267   306.874'30954—dc22   2006   2006020391

ISBN: 978-81-321-1134-4 (PB)

The SAGE Team: Anindita Majumdar, Rajib Chatterjee and Santosh Rawat

To our mothers, grandmothers, ourselves,
our children, their children—born or unborn . . . .

Contents

৵

OURSELVES

৵

OUR CHILDREN

Contents   9

❧

Foreword

❧❦

Motherhood Revisited

> *The boy asked his mother*
> *'Where did I come from*
> *Did you pick me up anywhere?'*
> *Mother replied, laughing and crying,*
> *Hugging the boy to herself*
> *'You were the desire in my heart.'*
> — Rabindranath Tagore
>
> *Mother and motherland*
> *Reign higher than Heaven.*
> — Saying in Sanskrit, often quoted in the
> literature of anti-colonial resistance

It is indeed with great pleasure and pride that I sit down to write this Foreword. Rinki Bhattacharya, after her visual forays into scenes depicting motherhood, has decided to address the issues of motherhood in print. She has chosen some of the stalwart feminist activists in the creative fields as well as critical, to focus on the issue experientially. Since experience is also the major critical tool in women's writing, the writings that have been gathered here by the editor, with a great deal of care and thoughtfulness, have also seen a lot of solid theorizing.

As I sit down to write this piece, I stare at two paintings by women, dealing with the theme of mother and child. In the first, the artist is a woman who brought up a son born out of wedlock, as a single parent. Whether it is a throwback to that or not, in it the mother–child symbiosis is depicted as one fraught with pain. In the other, painted by my daughter, I am portrayed as the disciplining mother making my rebellious daughter finish a piece of needlework. The composition brings out the mother–daughter dyad in its complexity.

Motherhood is a phenomenon of 'infinite variety' though, not infrequently, 'staled' by 'custom'. Yet, whether it is in myths or traditions or in scientifically inflected psychoanalysis, motherhood is one of the prime sites of reproduction. We must remember that it is not only the human species that is reproduced, but Motherhood and mothering themselves are reproduced (Chodorow 1978) to keep the patriarchal structure of society intact—to perpetuate the 'world-historical defeat of the female sex' (Engels 1972: 20). In modern Indian society, motherhood is one of the essentializing signifiers of womanhood and femininity. The present collection is a salutary pointer to the manipulation of the lives of women through this essentializing device. Far from being an unchanged static category, motherhood is capable of many permutations, refracting some of the major stratificatory categories. The position of motherhood in our understanding and experience of everyday predicaments is quite complex. Motherhood cannot be unduly glorified nor minimized in our commitment to feminist explorations of it. Let us, therefore, recapitulate some of the debates that have been thrown up by feminists since the 1970s.

A recent number of the British Council Newsletter *Connecting* mentions that the result of an extensive survey on the most beautiful and beloved word in English, has zeroed in on 'Mother'. I have a feeling that in other languages too this would be a likely finding. It is not for nothing that the editor of this collection has spoken of the mother–child relationship as 'the oldest love story'. The inevitability of the relationship, interestingly enough, also makes it one of the most controversial. For feminists in particular, Motherhood has meant both an unmistakable assertion of women's subjectivity and the most obvious capitulation to patriarchal ruling. What Catherine Mckinnon had said about sexuality and labour in the context of feminism and Marxism is truer than ever of Motherhood: that which is most her own, is most easily taken away. A woman's most obvious power to reproduce and nurture the species is then made into the most effective engine of her enslavement. This is one of the most central paradoxes of society that is camouflaged by the halo that usually surrounds motherhood.

The paradox is intensified in the situation of a slave woman whose motherhood is an intrinsic part of her enslavement. Such a voice is the famous one of Sojourner Truth, whose motherhood was indeed a precondition to her slavery, because apart from her productive labour, her reproductive labour was also part of the package of her enslavement.

> Look at me! Look at my arm! I have ploughed and planted, and gathered into barns, and no man could head me! And ain't I a woman? I could work as much and eat as much as a man—when I could get it—and bear the lash as well! And ain't I a woman? I have borne thirteen children, and seen most all sold off to slavery, and when I cried out with my mother's grief, none but Jesus heard me! And ain't I a woman? (Sojourner Truth 1851)

As it turned out, for class and caste-ridden societies, the hallmark of privilege lay with the women who were delinked from productive labour and relegated to the reproduction of status through procreation of species. In fact, I congratulate the compiler of the present volume for having chosen from among the multiple synonyms of 'mother' the word *Janani*, which denotes reproduction. The institutional build-up of Motherhood, whether through upper-caste rituals, especially when a woman fulfils the expectation of perpetuating the patrilineal clan by producing a son, or through the glowing effect of the white, well-fed mothers breast-feeding healthy babies with beatific smiles—are all ploys of reproducing the dominant patriarchal structure of privileges. Therefore, it is salutary to remember that underbelly of motherhood as experienced by the Black slave woman, before she was freed to be named Sojourner Truth.

The early engagement of Second Wave feminists with the theme of Motherhood, both in its theoretical aspect and in its institutional aspects was only to be expected, and these forays yielded memorable results. Adrienne Rich's *Of Women Born* (1977), which has been likened to Simone de Beauvoir's *The Second Sex* (1953) is a magnificent road map of the triumphs and travails of maternity. Nancy Chodorow's classic diagnosis (1978) brings out the necessity of our society to have Motherhood and mothering reproduced endlessly, so that it gets naturalized. What is very noteworthy is that the so-called traditional and so-called modern converge on the myth of motherhood because it appears to give the most effective boost to the patriarchal control over women—not just her body, but also her mind.

In the West, the Freudian revolution in designating a child's psychological development, according to later feminists, reinforced the nature–culture dichotomy—the mother standing for pre-civilizational nature. With their strong reading of Marx, both Mary O'Brien (1982) and Allison Jaggar (Jaggar and McBride 1989) have taken issue with Marx for having accepted the distinction between reproduction and production, with motherhood occupying the private domain as mere reproduction, whereas, history belongs to the public domain because that is the world of production and politics. Just as the socialization process is assigned, under the Freudian explanatory system, to the regime of the father, in an uncritical understanding of the Marxian system the domain of historical change is dominated by the male who clearly occupy the productive sphere.

Among traditional Hindu beliefs, Motherhood enters into a symbiosis with the world of goddesses, thereby drawing upon the mythical world. According to this mythical world, the mother goddess is called *Shakti* (energy), an imputed power is attributed to Motherhood. Yet, mothering is so far one of the most disempowering of social roles in traditional or poor families (Bagchi 2001). The ambivalence that surrounds motherhood appears to have a transcultural spread. Motherhood, thus, is a standard way of implementing authoritarian regimes, such as in imperializing countries. The Fascist agenda of Motherhood in the Fatherland is another such myth with which women and their wombs are targeted in order to reproduce domination (Haug 1988).

Stripped of this patriarchal aura, however, Motherhood and mothering do involve women's agency, her affective qualities and her desires and dreams. The myth and reality of Motherhood, therefore, offers a Gordian knot that is not easy to cut. As Mary O'Brien (1982) argued so forcefully, there is a willful degradation of women's reproductive function in the available theory of social reproduction:

> Women are evidently tied to nature by the a-human act of giving birth to humans. The unanimity and harmony of the male-voiced intellectual choir has had some curious and damaging effects. Simone de Beauvoir, for instance, despite the power and integrity in her work accepts without question the evaluation of childbirth as an inferior animal activity and the biological curse of femininity. (Ibid.: 104)

Mary O'Brien likewise critiques Shulamith Firestone's explanation of the biology-centredness of motherhood and agrees with Juliet Mitchell that replacing nature with technology, as Firestone suggests, is dualistic not dialectical and, therefore, simplistic (O'Brien 1982). Though contraception does revolutionize Motherhood in introducing the space for choice and volition into it, however, the power that it offers to women is limited, fraught as it is with notions of patriarchal control that wish to regulate paternity.

Private and Public

If the division between reproduction and production is fraught with dialectical tension, the division between private and public is equally fraught on the question of Motherhood and maternity. For all the privacy imputed to conception and childbirth, Motherhood is one of the most publicly-controlled institutions in modern and traditional societies, alike. Much of the most privately experienced anxieties are really played out overtly in the theatre of the public arena in life (Bagchi 1990).

If reproduction is so clearly relegated to the private sphere, why is population control so blatantly an area of public policy? The fact of the matter is that with all the confidence with which the 'modern' system of social organization tries to separate the public from the private, as soon as it comes to taking a close look at women's agency and what it can *produce*, the iron curtain between *private* and *public*, between *reproduction* and *production* breaks down to produce a continuum. Women's writing, like women's maternity, are as much part of the public sphere as political debates and state policies. The site of production in each case belongs to the private space of women—a corner in a room because she may not have a *room of her own*, or in the artificial seclusion of an *anturghar* or, at best in the segregated maternity ward of a hospital—but their impact on civil society is enormous. The science of demography is built around births, survivals, deaths. As this is the area in which the state tries to control births in the name of population control, Motherhood becomes captive to state control, often using coercive methods like the two-child norm for occupying public offices, including Panchayati Raj institutions. As the initial reaction of the majoritarian Hindutva forces to the early release of Census data broken up into different religious communities indicated, the fertility rate among women of minority communities poses a threat to communalist forces in the country. Both from the normative and transgressive points of view, therefore, women's wombs become major players in the power games of the nation-state.

మ

In the light of these severe contestations, these oscillations between power and powerlessness, the present collection of experiential narratives of motherhood takes on a dimension of extreme importance. The narratives clearly point towards the futility of homogenizing the notion of Motherhood, refracted as it is with multiple dimensions of this extremely close bonding— the 'oldest love story' as the editor has so movingly called it. These 19 odd narratives are from some of the best-known figures in women's movement and women's studies in contemporary India, who have opened their hearts, whether in recalling their experience of their own mothers, in reflecting on their own role as mothers, or in focusing as mothers on their children—biological or adoptive. Limited as the narratives are by class, this limitation is also the strength of the volume. It opens a window to the emerging class subjectivity of women from different parts of India, whose personal explorations of their varied sites of motherhood were clearly infused with their respective engagement with the politics of gender, at work within families. Personal, one has to admit while reading the essays, is political with a refreshing degree of subversive strategies at work, the most unforgettable being in C.S. Lakshmi's 'When Alamelu Shrugged' where the Alsatian's compliance with the taboos of a Brahmanical kitchen amounted simply to placing his back and tail outside it, similar to her mother's attempts at subverting the rules and taboos of the Brahmanical kitchen. Without giving too much emphasis to genealogy, however, one certainly sees where Ambai's strength came from.

Of the three sections Our Mothers, Ourselves and Our Children, the first is not only the largest, but also appeals to our affective sensibilities the most. Interestingly, it is also the most political of the three sections. The discovery of the potential bonding with one's mother definitely owes a great deal to the feminist upsurge through a new phase of the women's movement which, to use Maitreyi Chatterji's phrase, was also called the autonomous women's movement, that largely helped break the private–public divide in one's political thinking. It is Maitreyi Chatterji who openly theorizes this 'experience'.

As I became deeply involved in the women's movement, the scales fell away from my eyes. My mother emerged before me in a new light. I often wondered—did she get the space she wanted? Did she realize it was her right? Or had she succumbed in life making sacrifices because that was what was expected of her? I began to reflect about my mother's struggle from the time I could remember, her feisty fights, her total support to us—so that we, her daughters could enjoy a better life.

What Maitreyi articulates so openly occurs as a sub-text in many of the narratives under the cluster, Our Mothers. What Virginia Woolf called 'thinking through our mothers' was a political act where 'personal is political', because the positioning of our personae that propels us through our activist lives is a product of a struggle that is transmitted from one generation to the next through struggling mothers. This was the scaffolding that upheld the trilogy written by Ashapurna Debi,* the grand narrative of the emergence of modern Bengali women when women become the driving force of history.

Dhiruben Patel writes about the experience of mother-bonding without the agony of physical birthing. For her, motherhood is a special way of relating to others, children or grown-ups. She had brought tears to the eyes of her nephew who felt rejected because she had told an outsider that he was her brother's child, just like she brought tears to the eyes of her Irish-American writer daughter Patricia, German daughter, Gretel and the unnamed Himalayan daughter. Through several other striking examples, which may or may not be explained by the theory of reincarnation, she makes a general observation that is, however, entirely credible: 'The magic bond of motherhood at times is woven between two individuals without a biological relationship.' Her narration brings out the strange ways in which one can become a mother, irrespective of blood-ties and age. Is this a refraction of being one of the most widely respected Gujarati writers belonging to a previous generation?

The wide variety of experiences of motherhood are narrated in this volume by a score or so of women who have made distinctive marks in contemporary India through their chosen areas of creativity and criticality. For each, motherhood has left a mark of central importance in their world of cognition. The re-cognition of motherhood has, therefore, plucked major chords in their heartstrings, so that Motherhood has come alive in its multiple shapes and forms.

*Ashapurna Debi, famous Bengali writer is known for her trilogy—including *Subarnalata* and *Bakul Katha*.

For Neela Bhagwat, who interprets and enriches the world through her music, her own composition in Raga Durga stakes her claims that motherhood is the basis of all relationships, ever-present and an ever-changing presence:

Kabhi tum ho behena
Kabhi sakhi pyari
Kabhi balak ho bilkhat
Kabhi piyaa ki reet nyari.

(I see you at times in
my sister or my friend,
sometimes in my child
and at times in my lover.)

She sings with inspiration because *tum hi ho adhar mayi* (you are the basis, mother), *daras det paras karat* (you are seen and you are touched), *karuna hi teri reet* (compassion is your custom).

One of the most striking aspects of the section on Our Mothers is our sense of how the discovery of what mothers meant in these high-achieving women's lives, coincided in a strange kind of way with their moment of self-discovery and, therefore, was central to the process of self-empowerment. While this is most prominent in Maitreyi Chatterji's narrative, it is also present as a sub-text in Bharati Ray's account. Despite her unduly modest assumption of the epithet 'ordinary' both for herself and her mother, she did have an extraordinary mother, a gold medallist of Delhi University from Indraprastha College and a champion swimmer. The daughter, who visibly found it iniquitous that her mother should follow her husband like his shadow, not out of any Shastric compulsions, but out of love for him. She records the moment of 're-cognition' when the mother, old and infirm, confesses that she had, indeed, neglected herself. This is the moment of bonding that brings the feminist activist to the fore. Or, take the case of Urmila Pawar, one of the major Dalit writers of contemporary India, who records the moment of motherhood as the one when the frail mother gets up, unaided, from the shock of her last surviving son's death, to declare that in her eyes all children are equal. This was a feminist declaration, as her remaining children were all girls, of whom Urmila Pawar was one. Motherhood is de-essentialized by a number of women of capability and understanding. In the case of Roshan G. Shahani, the mother and mother-in-law bond is the most extraordinary way to com-municate the 'infinite variety' of expressions associated with motherhood. Tutun Mukherjee's recreation of Alice Walker's *In Search of Our Mother's Garden* (1999) in the beautiful embroidered creation of her mother, or in the veritable gardens she created out of her culinary skill, in the aroma of spices and the proportionately-cut vegetables is yet another affirm-ation of the 'different' ways by which creativity in mothers expressed itself.

This sentiment is corroborated in Dhiruben Patel's extraordinary ac-count of the intense bonding akin to motherhood, which she experienced without being a biological mother. Dhiruben Patel consoled Gretel, her daughter of 'brief encounter', with the Hindu belief in reincarnation; and Nita Ramaiya refused to take recourse to artificial insemination be-cause she believed it to go against the 'Indian' notion of married chastity! But it is made quite clear from the narrations across generations, regions and caste divides, that motherhood is so varied that it defies easy general-izations. Dhiruben Patel, for instance, refused to marry and enter into the agony and ecstasy of biological motherhood, but as said earlier, mother-hood came to her in the most extraordinary circumstances, sometimes even at the risk of being considered a witch with an evil eye!

In the section in which the authors focus on themselves, the experience of birthing comes through with poignancy and intensity. Kamala Das's briefly narrated experience is full of the rich sensuousness of the kind of care that is given to our girls only when they are glorified by child-birth. The novelist Shashi Deshpande is rightly bewildered by her attempts at deconstructing Motherhood. While she is openly contemptu-ous of those women who have fully internalized the stereotype of Mother-hood so that all their humanity (including sexuality, of course) is subsumed under motherhood, yet, she is uneasy when she resents her mother want-ing something for herself, or when she finds herself expecting too much from her own children because she is their mother! These unresolved issues haunt the narration of Shashi Deshpande, justifying her claim to fame as a novelist of repute in our times.

Pratibha Ranade, herself a well-known translator, discusses the see saw in the roles of motherhood, even the return of the role of disciplining that had once been repugnant to her. The chain of motherhood is, thus, not easily broken. Mallika Sarabhai, the talented artist that she is, writes a letter to her children, talking about her life—now and before, the break up with her husband, but most of all about her creative talents, which means long absences, away from them when she goes away to perform.

Motherhood, which posits its all-devouring attention on children, needs to be refurbished with time and space so that the mother can reflect and put her creative acts together; 'I yearn for solitude,' says Mallika the danse-use mother, 'and a tiny space of harmony within myself … I use the time to re-affirm my art and rekindle my values. Without this opportunity to be centred I would be a lesser mother to both of you.' Motherhood without the mother's selfhood is not complete. Painter Rekha Rodwittiya, on the other hand, brought up her son as a single parent for the first seven years of his life. For her, motherhood is not just a surrogate friendship but a distinctive relationship in which they are placed as mother and son. This, for instance, includes the pain of having to leave him with her mother to go to London and complete her Master's degree, or holding his little hands after he falls asleep to allay *her own* fear of the dark, or assigning a corner to him in her studio when she painted.

Nita Ramaiya has written of her experience of adoptive motherhood, its unexpected challenge without the long, slow preparation of pregnancy. But the challenges and joys experienced in motherhood are qualitative-ly no different, while they add newer dimensions. Nita Ramaiya's story talks of Aneri who named her adopted child *Jasud*, meaning hibiscus. Glowing in the self-chosen colour of the hibiscus, she felt 'empowered to the fullest!'. Daughter of an *Aparajita* (the alter ego of Nabaneeta's highly talented mother), Nabaneeta Dev Sen's irrepressible account of her mother-ing of three daughters, two biological and the third post-menopausal, hovers over all the three sections, though ostensibly belonging to the third. Holding her literary creativity in a symbiotic relationship with her mater-nity, Nabaneeta gives us the rare gift of the poetry of motherhood. The poems that she wrote to celebrate the birthing process have lent a unique dimension to her otherwise hard-hitting narrative. Nabaneeta Dev Sen's story of mothering has come across as a combination of buoyancy and weight that has enriched the entire volume.

It is to the credit of the editor that she has not shied away from the most resonating of absences. Deepa Gahlot's determination not to fall into the trap of motherhood, even an adoptive one, particularly when she was known for her ease in communication with articulate children, is a positive commentary on and not just a negative denial of the burden and social incongruity that has got built into the ways in which motherhood may be confronted. The volume, one feels, would have remained incom-plete without Anwesha Arya's own account of the termination of preg-nancy that she had to undergo, even though it might have been legal under the Medical Termination of Pregnancy (MTP) Act. Abortion, as the 'act' is generally called, is still such a surreptitious one that no visible support system is available for these vulnerable mothers whose birthing is cruelly halted. Such a poignant confessional piece has completed the process of de-essentializing Motherhood in the modern Indian context.

Thus, meandering through motherhood, these remarkable women touch the core of their capability and creativity. That motherhood elicits these varied and rich responses in these women is a testimony to its durability within fragility, power within powerlessness (Krishna Raj 1995).

— JASODHARA BAGCHI

References

Bagchi, Jasodhara. 1990. 'Representing Nationalism: The Ideology of Mother-hood in Colonial Bengal', *Economic and Political Weekly*. WS 20–27.

———. 2001. 'From Heroism to Empowerment: Identity and Globality among the Slum Women of Khidirpur', *Identity Locality and Globalization. Experiences in India and Indonesia*. New Delhi: ICSSR.

Chodorow, Nancy. 1978. *The Reproduction of Mothering*. Berkeley: University of California Press.

De Beauvoir, Simone. 1953. *The Second Sex*. New York: Alfred Knopf.

Engels, Frederick. 1972. *On the Origin of Family Private Property and the State*, ed. Eleanor B. Leacock. New York: International Publications Co. (First Published 1884).

Haug, Frigga. 1988. 'Mothers in Fatherland'. *New Left Review*. November–December.

Jaggar, Alison M. and William L. McBride. 1989. 'Reproduction as Male Ideology', in *Women's Studies International Forum*. Special Issue featuring *HYPATIA*, Pergamon Press.

Krishna Raj, Maithreyi. 1995. 'Motherhood, Power and Powerlessness', in Jasodhara Bagchi (ed.), *Indian Women, Myth and Reality*. Hyderabad: Orient Longman.

O'Brien, Mary. 1982. 'Viewpoint Feminist Theory and Dialectical Logic', in Nannerl O. Keohane, Michelle Z. Rosaldo and Barbara C. Gelpi (eds), *A Critique of Ideology*. University of Chicago: Harvester Press.

Rich, Adrienne. 1977. *Of Woman Born. Motherhood as Experience and Institution*. London: Virago Press.

Sojourner Truth. 1797–1883. Ain't I A Woman? Speech delivered in 1851 at the Women's Convention, Akron, Ohio, USA. http://www.fordham.edu/halsall/mod/sojtruth-woman.html. Accessed 13 March 2005.

Preface

Janani was a spontaneous response to our anxious mood—particularly mine—more than a decade and a half back. I remember it being a curiously bewildering phase. A period when I was beginning to feel excluded from the mainstream activities of my own family. But, it took me a foolishly long time to realize that I had been practically 'retired' as a mother. My retirement, however, brought none of the benefits one associates with several years of dedicated service. Nor had I transformed overnight into a gray-haired venerable elder. For sometime, I hung around like a solitary note after the orchestra ensemble falls silent.

Used to a bustling home, being at the beck and call of the children, I seemed redundant and sadly, unwanted. This phase has been referred to as the 'empty nest' period—when children, like birds, have flown away by simply growing up. It was abundantly clear that my children no longer needed a mother. Except on rare occasions. I was not required on a minute-to-minute basis. Locked as women are, in their traditional mothering images, Indian mothers refuse to believe that children, at all, grow up. Few women accept the fact of ever becoming redundant to their beloved children. Mothers encounter traumatic experiences, as a result. Sometimes this can adversely affect the relationship between mothers and children—often leaving permanent scars.

I admit being completely disoriented and bruised for a considerably long period of time … indeed it took me years to recover from this sense of rejection. I wonder at times, if I have recovered fully. Recently, I was watching the exquisitely crafted film biography of James M. Barrie (the creator of Peter Pan) titled *Finding Neverland* with the dashing Johnny Depp portraying the writer, Barrie. In one unforgettable scene he wistfully says: '*Children should never be sent to bed, they wake up one day older and before we know they are grown up*', expressing sentiments most mothers would endorse!

In addition to being a retired mother, by the early 1990s, I had earned the dubious distinction of being divorced and single. The social isolation produced by this lethal combination was claustrophobic, to say the least. On the positive side, many of my friends were speedily 'retiring' as mothers. Some of our children had migrated abroad. Others had moved on in life. They—the children—had literally performed vanishing acts. But if any one of us was going through unbearable pangs of separation, that pain was stifled, or hidden successfully, from others. We concealed our throbbing pain, the inevitable emptiness, wearing a mask of carefully constructed nonchalance. A few of us had been actively associated with the autonomous women's movement. Our exposure to women's issues brought a certain edge to understanding the harsh reality of women—or mothers—in similar situations. Urmila (Pawar) has repeatedly observed in her narrative, 'The Cross a Woman Carries' about women being perceived as having neither existence nor identity except as a mother. In Mahashweta Devi's collection, *In the Name of the Mother* (2004) there is one story titled 'Ma from Dawn to Dusk'. Her eloquent title affirms that women are nothing but mothers.

Ancient people once referred to all females as 'mother'. This was prompted by their reverence for the wonderful capacity women possess to create people—'*a miracle all women and only women are able to perform, whether or not we do so*'. There is little shift in this universal perception about women. In this system, women can rarely hope to escape motherhood if they were to wish it.

That was, however, entirely untrue about the women who eventually constructed *Janani*. None of us were *merely* Mothers. Nor were we those eternally sobbing, sacrificing stereotypes of mothers thrown up routinely on the Bollywood screen! Even at the bleakest time, I had at least one newspaper column to write for. Amongst the other retiring mothers were many stalwarts—eminent writers, performing artists, activists and foremost feminist scholars in creative fields as well as critical. Each one had secured a niche. This, I consider one of the most fascinating and important aspects of *Janani*.

Unredeemed loneliness, I think, has the uncanny knack of ushering in the creative process. The process begins once we acknowledge that things could not get any worse. And this book is a living testimony to the fact that out of a deep chasm of pain emerge works of great significance. One of the ploys I engaged in to silence my own growing loneliness was to discreetly plan 'tea' at home. I would invite some of the retired mothers who were after all, dear friends. Soon these 'tea' sessions at home turned into a lively forum. At the informal forum our grievances—even anger—could be voiced or the emotional vacuum filled—even if briefly.

At one of these meetings, I remember casually suggesting that we ought to register our frustrations, anger, confusion and conflicting thoughts about motherhood in general and link it to our personal experiences. In other words, make honest observations about the way women feel once their children move on. Every time our little group met—often without agenda—we bonded closer. Frequent rounds of mint tea and savories, revived our spirits. We talked of issues close to our heart. Attention was drawn to the lonely course motherhood had taken and our concern about women's redundancy as 'mothers' (parents in general) soon overtook others concerns. Many of us even wondered if motherhood was not strictly a duty without rights or rewards?

When *Janani* tentatively started, none of the writers had the slightest notion about the fate of our essays. But the idea was enthusiastically greeted. As already mentioned, none of the women were *merely* housewives nor mothers. Each of us had a distinct professional identity—for example, Navjot was a well-known, contemporary painter (she dropped out later), Neela Bhagwat—an accomplished *khayal* exponent and Urmila was a highly regarded Dalit writer. Dhiruben was the most acclaimed and inspirational figure amongst us. Interestingly, she is the only non-biological mother writing on motherhood. Dhiruben cheerfully argues that, to be a mother, one does not have to actually give birth! She is not the only practitioner of that belief. In the Indian joint family system—childless widows often became surrogate mothers, as do unmarried aunts. The practice continues. These women were no less loving than biological mothers.

The meeting that led to the idea of expressing our thoughts on motherhood was a definitive moment. It helped lay down the cornerstone for this fine collection. As the idea of documenting our thoughts came in an instant—so did the essays. Following this, in the second meeting, we decided to request others—distinguished women who had chosen their vocations, their destiny ... dancers, writers, activists, painters, poets—to join the book project to share their personal experiences of motherhood and daughterhood. I doubt the two can be separated into watertight compartments—both constantly interface, clash, or compliment and nurture one another—what Virginia Woolf refers to as 'thinking through our mothers'.

Without further delay, I dispatched requests to various friends. Many of the essays arrived in less than a week. The first essay came from Kamala Das. Shashi Despande's persuasive piece, 'Learning to be a Mother' followed. Mallika (Sarabhai) and Rekha (Rodwittiya) responded at once. The collection, now grew in volume. These essays and those by Jyotsna Kamal and Pratibha Ranade belong to the early phase—roughly 1994–95. But like *Behind Closed Doors* (2004), I had to put *Janani* into cold storage. Until the release and subsequent recognition of my above book on domestic violence—the *Janani* manuscript continued to languish.

During the Kolkata book release of *Behind Closed Doors* in June 2004, I met Bharati Ray. I casually mentioned working on a collection of essays titled *Janani* to Bharatidi, who seemed greatly interested. She required little convincing and her moving essay arrived in a matter of weeks. By then Sage had expressed positive interest in the project, which was indeed heartening news. So, I boldly invited several writers of repute— Roshan G. Shahani, Nabaneeta Dev Sen, Nita Ramaiya, C.S. Lakshmi to join the project. Meanwhile, Dr Jasodhara Bagchi agreed to write the Foreword. Even after her Foreword was dispatched, two of our contributors—the youngest of the lot, a journalist colleague Deepa (Gahlot) and my daughter Anwesha (Arya), wanted to contribute. Without hesitation, I welcomed them. Both delve into deeply disturbing—in fact, the darker side—of motherhood. Deepa's *piece de resistance* audaciously defends a woman's decision to remain child-free in a society where such a decision invites ridicule, not respect. But Deepa represents the new-age woman. She draws our attention to a common burden mothers carry— that of guilt. Deepa's personal struggle against conformity, her decision to remain childless, is the only voice *against* motherhood.

And Anwesha's poignant account arrived when the book had left my desk for the publishers. Her essay on the unspeakable—'abortion'—is filled with the desperate unhappiness of a young girl whose journey to motherhood was stonewalled by social censure. By a joyous coincidence she is about to be the mother of her first born. Tutun's (Mukherjee) evocative essay was delayed by the sad demise of her mother and my friend Maithili (Rao) graciously agreed to join last month—her piece completes *Janani*'s charmed circle.

The essays view motherhood from a spectrum of kaleidoscopic perspectives. Many of the authors pay belated homage to their mothers. Is it not a tragic irony that we take our own mothers for granted during their lifetime and value them too late? Fewer write about their children and lesser number of writers turn their inner eye on themselves. It is the two younger authors who air their views about unconventional personal choices and their headlong clash with traditional ideas of motherhood. Experience is considered a major critical tool in women's writing. All these essays, in dwelling on important issues experientially, hold the mirror to our cultural legacy.

However, none of the authors enter into the grave issue of Indian society's condemnation of women who fail to give birth to children. Nor is there any debate on how childless women are routinely ill-treated as inauspicious creatures, especially seen in their exclusion from most fertility rites. Also, the portrait of mothers who burn their young daughters-in-law, is absent from this picture gallery. But patriarchal ideology blames women for all their misfortunes. They are tortured or abandoned if they do not give birth to sons, or on other pretexts. These issues deserve our vigilante attention, some day, in another volume.

Despite the hard and endless struggle involved—or perhaps because of it—I was determined to get this marvellous anthology published. With my terrible track record of losing important documents—passports, cheque books, ration cards—it is nothing short of a miracle that the earlier essays survived. Our collective work, rejected several times by important publishers and after languishing for nearly a dozen years, is unbelievably, coming out of the shadows.

I am grateful to those friends who encouraged me—particularly Asha Damle. And I am immensely fortunate for the support of my contributors and my publishers, Sage Publications India.

Our Mothers

My Mother

❧❧

Bharati Ray

If you want to know who the real heroes of world history are,
just look at the mothers.
— Peter Hoeg, Danish author

'Come, please. Her condition is critical. No, do not rush. But you need to come.' The almost-expected telephone call came from the Calcutta Hospital. My brother, Abhijit, his wife and I left our breakfast table and rushed to the ICU where Mother had been lying for over a fortnight, fighting for her life. Before stepping out of the lift, my brother said, 'I don't want her to die now.' I stroked his cheeks, 'Let her go, Abhijit,' I said gently.

We entered the hospital room. She was already gone—she must have already passed away when they called. My brother and his wife, who had come from abroad to be by her side during her last days, were looking intently at her face, grief-stricken and overwhelmed.

So, she is gone, I thought. I remembered the days when I used to sit by her bedside, and she used to fondly stroke my arms with her feeble hands, and bless me again and again. She was so happy that I looked after her and cared for her. Did she know what I used to think? Could anyone guess? While everyone tried to feed her *rasogollas* (which she loved), make her smile and take every care so that she could live longer, I alone sat and prayed, 'Take her away, dear God!,' this was no living. Living was humiliating. To depend on others for feeding, bathing and changing soiled beds, again and again! I did not want such a living for myself and not for my mother either. Everyone would have been shocked had I told them what I thought, while caressing her face. They all said, 'She is with us. She talks, she jokes, she eats.' The *ayah*s were happy, they were getting their salaries and the patient was undemanding, my *mashima* was comfortable with her sister for company, my sister Tapati was pleased that she still had a *baper bari*. Pronoti, the youngest and the sweetest of us three sisters, believed our mother was a protecting angel. All our other relatives wished her to get well and live long out of the respect they bore for my father. I alone wished her dead!

Did I then not love my mother? I had always thought that I did not love her enough. I only did my duty towards her, being the eldest child and the best placed to do so. She was almost ninety, thin, emaciated and ugly, without a single tooth, with shrunken skin, swollen eyes and was a victim of Parkinson's.

I remember her when she and I were both younger. No, I did not love her, but I was proud of her. She was very beautiful and smart, had graduated from Indraprastha College, Delhi University, in 1934, with a gold medal (which she bequeathed to me) for standing first among girls and had mathematics and economics as her subjects. Brought up in a well-to-do *mamabari* (my grandmother was just a 14-year-old girl at the time of my mother's birth) along with *mama*s, all of them very bright and vivacious, my mother, Kalyani, was spoilt and loved by all. The whole world seemed to be at her feet. She was happy and had all she thought she wanted.

Then she got married, and made her first and crucial mistake. She fell head over heels in love with my father. He was a rather remarkable man in every sense, I agree, but as our ancient *Shastras* wisely warn, '*sarbam atyantam garhitam*'—too much of anything is bad. To love your husband may be all right, but to be overpowered by that love and forget yourself totally, give up your individuality, is no good. My mother did that. She lived like a shadow of my father. No, not because she was a devout Hindu, or because the *Shastras* prescribed a woman to be *patibrata*. Religion, based on so-called *Shastras*, and my mother were poles apart. But love is love. And while loving our father, she never pursued further studies, or thought of carving out a life, or developing hobbies of her own. We two sisters came along and she—not a besotted but sensible mother—taught us at home, sewed our dresses, cooked in the *niramish* kitchen for my *thakurma* and *pishima* who always stayed with us, in the *niramish* kitchen and looked after the streams of guests who thronged our home. I remember while we were five of us—three sisters and our parents—our father was posted in Kurseong in the district of Darjeeling—we had 36 guests at the same time at our house. Everyone in the extended family seemed to be in poor health and in need of a change of air. My mother, always a gentle, soft-spoken person—never shouted, never lost her temper, never talked much and never expressed any annoyance. Simple food—*dal*, one *sabji* and a fish curry—was served to all. Beds were made on *madurs* and *satranchis* on the floor, pillows hastily made with old clothes, pushed into old cushion covers and thick *kanthas* sewn with old sarees (blessed be that craft!) were offered to protect them from the cold. Those who came—mainly our relations—ate, slept, roamed about in the hills, and were unanimous in their praise of my father. His generosity—he was generous—his charming manners, they were charming indeed, his witty conversation, he was a gifted conversa-tionalist—delighted all. The elders blessed him and the young, admired him. No one said much to my mother or about her.

We two sisters, Tapati and I (Pronoti came 10 years later and Abhijit even later) by mutual consent divided our parents between us. *Baba* was mine, *Ma*—Tapati's. As sisters we were very close and loving. I do not think *Baba* treated us differently from each other (Tapati may think other-wise), but I always felt my mother did. Perhaps because Tapati was weaker of the two, was thin and often sick, perhaps because our relatives favoured me above her, *Ma* was protective of Tapati. Once when we were in Patuakhali in the district of Barisal, my mother stitched a shirt and a pair of trousers exclusively for Tapati. I watched her for days sewing with great care and with great love, only for Tapati (so it seemed to me). When it was done, a beautiful set, I could take it no more. As she left the room, I brought out her pair of scissors and made an inch-deep cut in the red-striped shirt. My mother came back all smiles, ready to take the trial fitting of my sister and her expression changed. Rarely did I see such anger on her face. She gave me a tight slap, and said, 'CHHI! You are jealous. Jealousy is a sin.' That was the first and the last time my mother ever slapped me. I was six. I was shocked. No, I was sure I did not love her.

Yet, I was proud. My friends were envious. 'You have a graduate mother who teaches you. That is why you are so good at maths.' 'Yes,' I would proudly assert, 'She was first in maths in Delhi University, don't you know?' 'Your translations are so good, and précis of such high standard', my classmates would comment, in the small-town schools I studied in. I would accept the compliment and smugly say, 'My mother teaches me. She studied in Delhi and is a gold medallist from Delhi University—don't you know?' As if it was their duty to know!!

My mother had a considerable number of qualities for me to brag about to my friends. She was an outstanding swimmer, who crossed the Ganga at Berhampore in Murshidabad (where her parents stayed) in record time and was a gifted athlete who delighted in playing badminton (tennis had not gained popularity then) with my father's male friends as partners or opponents, a woman of outstanding physical courage and the coolest of nerves, that was evident every time there was a family crisis, be it a riot (during those red days in the 1940s) or my father's serious illness. Yet, instead of developing any of her skills, she chose to become a housewife. Did she really choose? Or, did she just give in to circumstances? I believe thinking was not her favourite pastime. Eating was, as was going out. There was not much scope for either, but she managed to do a little of both.

She was fond of finery too. But she could not manage it. In our conservative family, no woman over forty wore coloured *saris*. She gave up wearing them when she touched forty. I remember her wearing a night-blue printed chiffon *sari* and long *jaroa* peacock-designed hanging earrings, gifts from her parents. When these faded, she did not buy any to replace them. For one thing, there was never money at home, and for another my widowed *thakurma* and *pishima* lived with us. Though my *thakurma* had four sons, each as fond of her as the other (an extremely lucky mother she was), she openly said, she preferred to live with the youngest because she loved him the most and because his wife was *saral* and *sada satyabadi* and therefore, needed looking after! My *thakurma* did not run the household, my mother did. *Thakurma* had no reason to take the trouble. She was extremely intelligent and knew that her slightest wish would get top priority in our home. She was not unkind to my mother. *Pishima* was. Throughout the day, she used to criticize her and find fault with her for almost everything. One day I became particularly annoyed because *Pishima* was uncharitably harsh to Mother. *Ma* had used what she considered the wrong hand, the right hand instead of the left, because the former had become *eto* or polluted—for the *pital-handi* she was cooking in. When my mother came out of the *niramish* kitchen, I sermonized, 'You have been cooking the whole morning, and she, sitting by your side, is merely criticizing. You know one should not be unjust, but should not put up with injustice either, as Rabindranath Tagore said. If you do not protest, I will give her a piece of my mind, much though I love her.' My mother took me aside to her room and in a deeply emotional voice said, 'Don't do that, Bharati, and do not ever utter such words about her. She is *dookhi*. We do not discuss her life. Do you know about it? She was married young into a very well-to-do family because of her exquisite beauty [It's true. She was stunning even at fifty.], but she became a widow when she was only nineteen. And, at that tender age, she had to lead the harsh life of a Hindu widow. She had only a son to give her comfort in a conservative and unloving *sasurbari*. Few families treat a widow well, especially if she is beautiful, they make her feel responsible for her husband's death. When her son turned twenty-one and she started hoping for a better life, he died suddenly of a two-day ailment. It was then that she left her *sasurbari* and came to live with us, penniless and childless. Do you want to add to her misery? I would not do that. Let her take out her frustrations, her pains on me. I do not mind. I understand. *And I want you to understand.*' Her last few words were uncharacteristically strong.

Everyone in the extended family greatly admired my father. He looked after relatives and people from the village in Dhaka to which he mentally belonged. If a niece became widowed, her family would be his concern; his *jamaibabu* died in a communal riot, automatically my father's sister and her children's education would be his responsibility; the thatched roof of my *thakurma*'s *guru* had perished in a fire, it was his duty to replenish it. Consequently, we never had money at home. As mother ran the household and my father entrusted his entire income to her, we used to think that she was thrifty.

Since I never thought highly of her, I was rude, disobedient and impatient with her. Only on two occasions did I feel close to her—during the birth of my two daughters. They say in Bengal that you can only repay your mother when you become a mother yourself—only then can one understand the pains of motherhood! The third time I felt close to her was during her last bout of illness—when she was dying. It was only after her death that I realized that throughout my life I had loved her dearly and had depended on her psychologically.

'I want to marry him, mother.'

'Yes, you will.' She, forever gentle, was firm in her support and I made a beautiful marriage.

'Which school do I put my daughter in, *Ma*?' I had studied in a Bengali-medium school, while English-medium schools were coming into fashion. She advised and the school proved to be just right for my daughter.

Now the ever-silent, never-demanding, rock-stable woman is gone. I thought I did not love her during her lifetime. I love her in her death.

My mother was not a famous person whose biography I can write as a historian, she did not build any institution that I can carry on in her memory after her death, she did not bequeath a large legacy to me that I can enjoy. She was a middle-class housewife—ordinary, if judged by ordinary standards—and a mother of ordinary middle-class children. She did not have high ambitions. She had one secret desire, which one day she revealed to me. She wanted to be loved.

It was difficult for my mother to be loved by people she met in the course of her normal daily chores or by the numerous relations she entertained at her home. She had one great failing. She could not tell a lie!!! If you want to be loved by people, you have to be a saint, like Mother Teresa; if you want to acquire popularity, you need to know how to 'act' (read pretend) a little, affect smiles when you don't feel like it and make exuberant manifestations of your affection for others. Popularity is easy to get, if you know how to, and if you are not stubborn, as mother was, about not telling a single word of white or black lie. Love, of course, is different from popularity. My mother wanted love—in her unassuming way—she did not get it from many people. I did not give it to her either. I could not say, '*Ma*, we all love you. I love you dearly.' Because I did not love her during her lifetime—I only love her after her death.

During the last phase of her illness, when I drew close to her, and we got talking one day, I asked her a very private question. 'Tell me, *Ma*, so that I can learn from you, what do you think is the greatest mistake you made in your life.' After a moment's hesitation, came the response, 'I never looked after myself.' A few moments later, she continued, 'Your father did not neglect me. Nor did any one else. I neglected myself. I was pretty, I did not try to maintain my looks, I was gifted in many ways and I did not nurture my gifts. I could speak (she meant oratory) and write, I could cycle and swim, I loved mathematics and solving mathematical problems. I could excel in culinary art as well as in dressmaking and designing. I never tried. I had many ambitions and some potential, but I never worked to realize any. I have not done my duty to myself.' The truth, the realization and the pain when all of it was too late!

I am a mother, too. I carved out a life different from my mother's. Unlike her, I planned and I organized. I knew what I wanted and worked towards it. I gave time and thought to my children and did what I considered was good for them. But was it good enough? More importantly, was it what they wanted?

It is difficult for one age group to feel the pulse of another age group, older or younger. Each generation has its distinctive values and ideals, its own gods and anti-gods, its idiosyncratic faiths and superstitions, its singular trajectories.

When I am gone, will my children say, 'We thought we did not love our mother during her life? we love her in her death?' Or, will they say, 'We loved our mother so—during her lifetime. In her death ....'

I do not know.

My Mother, My Daughter

ಳಿ

Maitreyi Chatterji

In a child's lunch box
A mother's thoughts.
—Japanese proverb

In Bengali Hindu homes, we grow up hearing heroic stories of mother-hood. This is of course not unique to any particular religion or culture. But I can speak only of Bengal. The themes of visual arts—I am mainly referring to Jamini Roy's[1] Mother and Child images—represent mother-hood. In Sculptor Meera Mukherjee's[2] bronze mother, the woman spreads her arms to shelter the child. Amongst the childhood stories I recall fondly, many are of famous sons, including tales of both Gods and mortals. Vidyasagar's[3] story of braving the dangerous Damodar river on a stormy night to keep a promise to his mother was given to us as a unique example of heroism. We have that popular mythological story about Goddess Durga's[4] two sons, Ganesh and Kartik.[5] These stories of devoted sons proving their *matri bhakti*—were our childhood favourites. It's also common for Bengalis to refer to their mothers as *Matri Devi*. Saint Ramakrishna[6] and the poet Ramprasad[7] were both ardent worshippers of the Mother Goddess. Motherhood may have been pitched to an exalted position, but the ground reality for Indian mothers is an entirely different matter. India's high maternal mortality rate and chronic malnutrition makes a mockery of motherhood myths ... yet we find women legitimize motherhood through acts of immense sacrifice. Indian mothers eat last or not at all. And of course, the Government's main target in family planning schemes promoting unsafe sterilizations are inevitably unsuspecting young mothers. Women go through multiple pregnancies to continue the male family line or risk abortions if the fetus is female ... are women in India able to sustain—or alter—motherhood myths of end-less sacrifice? The answer to that question blows in the wind.

All this of course brings to mind my dear mother—or simply *Ma*. Our relationship was a finely-layered one. The first vivid memory I have of *Ma* is the sweet fragrance of Tata Eau de Cologne soap. And the familiar aroma of the spirit lamp greeted us on all train journeys. *Ma* liked us to be clean and she was most particular about what we ate. No street food or anything from the station platforms ... never. Our childhood memories are inextricably linked to a cane basket filled with food for train journeys, together with a large flask of warm water. Most trips *Ma* undertook with us were on her own. Our headmaster father rarely got permission for leave from school. On the Kolkata visits, *Mama* received us at the station. But on our Jaipur trips—where Mother's older sister lived, an escort was a dire necessity. There were no direct trains those days—we had to alight at either Tundla or Old Delhi. It was a pretty hazardous journey for a single woman with four infants between the ages of six and one.

The other recurring image from childhood is *Ma* telling us stories. These were not very frequent occasions as she had plenty of housework to absorb her. But *Ma* helped me with Bengali spellings, besides encouraging me to read. When we were growing up, a child's world was tightly sealed from that of adults. We were not supposed to be present at adult chat sessions. In our TV-free and radio-frequented childhood, neighbourhood women would gather at a particular house to exchange gossip, or share recipes till the children returned home from school. In winter, these *adda*s shifted to the warm courtyards bathed in mellow sunshine. Sometimes the women would go to a nearby temple. *Ma* was a part of this group and yet she seemed a shade different. What precisely that difference was, remains a mystery. It is possible we were too young to fathom its nuances. But I must confess we were mighty proud of our mother.

One of our favourite childhood pastimes was to flick through illustrated Bengali annuals. Pictures of goddesses, queens, fairies—in our eyes looked like our mother. Delighted, we would scream '*mago mani, mago mani*' (mother darling). We made such a racket that *Baba* had to come out of his study just to scold us for making a noise.

I was born with a congenital heart defect—actually a hole in the heart. When this was detected at age three months, the family doctor predicted an early end to my life. However, somehow I managed to live. It was only at the age of nine that I was permitted to attend school. Till that happened, I, with my siblings, studied at home, though my brother attended the boys' school where Father was the headmaster. Apart from studies, I spent most of the time inventing various pranks with a string of devoted followers and *Didi*, who lead us like the Pied Piper of Hamlin. There was a small water body outside our house. During the monsoons, the pit got filled up with enough water to splash around but not drown us. I remember, the film on the 1948 Olympic games had just been released. The Olympics swimming event and the long distance events fired our imagination. The water body became our swimming pool and running around the courtyard, our racetrack. One morning, after Mother had dutifully bathed us, I had the sudden urge to enact the Olympics swimming event. Out of the house I ran, followed by others. We splashed happily making a sorry mess of our clean clothes. When *Ma* came to call us for lunch naturally she did not find anyone in the house. Our gleeful shouts brought her out. She almost fainted with shock and anger on seeing our state. Identified as the ringleader, I was of course, justly spanked. Our next athletic feat was the run. It was fun to run all over the courtyard with wet bodies. Again poor *Ma* had to tidy the mess left by a trail of soapy water and wet running feet.

School put an end to our fun and games. The school bus stopped at our door sharp at eight. We were bathed, dressed in clean clothes, ready with tiffin carriers and water flasks. *Ma* would cook a simple meal of *dal*, *bhat* and *tarkari*, feeding us well. We never missed the school bus. No small achievement in our pre-refrigerator, pre-LPG or pressure cooker childhood. A big shed in school became our lunch room. Five days a week *Ma* packed five different menus. Maitreyi and Madhumati's (sister's) tiffin became the talk of the class. Somehow this news reached the ears of the nuns. Four nuns were assigned bus duty—a pair in the morning and in the evening. One morning, Sister Hilda expressed her wish to see *Ma*. I was awfully nervous because I continued playing pranks even in school. However, the next morning *Ma*, after much reluctance, stood quietly on the steps of the school verandah. Sister Hilda greeted her with a smiling *namaste.*

'We admire you for being such a good mother. Do you have a cook to help?', she asked *Ma.* The sister was amazed to hear that *Ma* did everything single-handed. After this incident all the bus nuns took turns to do their respectful *namaste* to *Ma.*

In my adolescent years there was a brief period when I frequently disagreed with *Ma.* This was mainly due to the fact that she disapproved of my friendship with certain girls in school or college. Life at school was particularly difficult when *Baba* heard from a fellow principal of another local school that my best friend was an extremely flirtatious girl. Sufficiently concerned, *Baba* consulted *Ma* about it. Matters came to a head when I requested *Ma's* permission to spend a weekend with the suspect friend at the school boarding-house. I had obtained written permission from the Mother Superior. Anyway, I spend that Easter vacation with my flirtatious best friend. When I returned home, *Ma* was terribly angry and refused to talk to me. This lasted for a week till I broke down.

College had its own set of problems. I was friendly with a girl who had the most terrible reputation in town. Even at that age she was the companion of a married man. A lively person, this girl was good fun to be with. I was really angry with *Ma* for showing disapproval. Most of the time *Baba* took her side asking me to respect *Ma's* wishes.

In my twentieth year, I left home for my postgraduate studies. Very soon, I had secured a job and met my future husband at the workplace. There was stiff opposition from my father's relatives to our marriage. We were *Vaidya*s by caste and my husband was a Brahmin. After some initial resistance, Mother's family accepted my choice and stood by us. Through out this period, as in my girlhood, I thought nothing about *Ma's* exceptional support—I took it naturally, for granted. Were not all mothers expected to support their children?

After his paralytic stroke, *Baba* was bed-ridden for seven-and-half-years till his death—making *Ma* a widow at fifty-three. The period after *Baba's* death was particularly hard for *Ma.* She took charge of our bereaved family. She had, in fact, to take most decisions during *Baba's* illness. However, officially *Baba* was regarded as the *karta* or head of the family. An affectionate man, *Baba* had a strong personality and rarely displayed his true emotions. He lost his mental strength after the stroke, becoming entirely dependent on *Ma*. His mere presence, I think, boosted *Ma's* courage. I observed her closely during *Baba's* illness. By this time, we had grown more intimate. *Ma* treated me as her sole confidante. *Ma's* widowhood made her increasingly dependent on me. But we continued to regard her as the family elder and decision maker.

At the young age of twenty-one, my second sister passed away. I am still astonished about the fact that *Ma* never broke down in spirit after the traumatic loss of a young daughter or at our father's stroke, or on seeing two sons divorced for that matter. After all that, she had only one goal in life—to get my youngest sister married. Ours was never a cash-rich household but I do not recall experiencing any kind of insecurity as a result. *Ma* would fret at times, saying she was not likely to get peace even after her death unless this daughter married. When my sister finally got married, *Ma* was visibly relaxed. After that she was a regular visitor to our Kolkata homes.

Sadly, by the year 1986, all that changed. *Ma* became critically ill. Our Hazaribagh sister-in-law was rather an uncaring sort of person. One of my brothers brought *Ma* down to Kolkata, with the precise idea that she would live with his family. As though overnight, *Ma* was uprooted from her rightful position as the head of the family. Her husband's home had been her home. In her son's house *Ma* was more a guest—albeit a welcome one—but it rankled her. The grandson born after her arrival became the apple of *Ma's* eye. She would offer them guidance, or suggestions—that were not always welcome or heeded—but *Ma* was no longer the sole decision-maker. I tend to believe she was deeply hurt but concealed the fact.

Her sudden decline in status was very hard for *Ma* to accept. For emotional support she turned more and more to me. Unknown to me, at some point of time *Ma* had become like my daughter. I could see my girlhood and youth reflected in her. Now, it was I who cajoled her to eat, take her medicines on time and advise her in our family matters, while she continued to guide my Bengali reading. I scoured book fairs or shops for books of different flavours that would please *Ma*. As long as she was fit enough to cook, *Ma* was fine. A time came when she was too frail to handle kitchen chores. *Ma* felt she was a burden on us. I would try to reason with her, as we tried our best to make her accept the inevitable frailty of age.

The last three years of *Ma's* life was spent with me and Kishore (my husband). During this period, I realized that she was the child I never had. I bathed and combed her hair, the way she had when I was in school or college. These were once a daily ritual for *Ma*. She would sit with a comb in hand—gently rub oil on my scalp before making neat braids.

Fifty years later, I was repeating the exact rituals for my mother. At times I had to scold *Ma* or act strict if she refused to drink Horlicks, her fruit juice or take proper nourishment. Like a child, *Ma* would turn to me for emotional support.

I joined the Autonomous Women's Movement in the early 1980s. For me, this was an important turning point of my life. That 'defining moment' you might say, to quote Henri Cartier Bresson.[8] I knew at once my life's calling. I identified women's problem in areas never before imagined. The most important issue before us was an individual's need for his or her own space—a room of one's own, however, clichéd the expression. As I became deeply involved in the women's movement, the scales fell away from my eyes. My mother emerged before me in a new light. I often wondered—did she get the space she wanted? Did she realize it was her right? Or had she succumbed to a life of making sacrifices because that was what was expected of her? The big question for me was to identify spaces denied to women. The women's movement was not just about anger or militancy. The movement made women search for their real identity. I began to reflect about my mother's struggle from the time I could remember, her feisty fights, her total support to us—so that we, her daughters, could enjoy a better life.

All her life, *Ma* had a tremendous fascination for the printed word. This was uncommon in the third decade of the 19th century. At that time, daughters were given no special status and marriage was considered a daughter's only destiny. I heard from others that *Ma* loved going to school. But she was unceremoniously withdrawn from Class VIII to care for my grandmother, who had uterine cancer. Grandma was never admitted to a hospital. Nor was a special nurse engaged for her. *Ma* must have missed school so much that she took to reading. Her reading habit survived. She was not interested in marrying a rich man, but she just wanted a *vidyan* husband. Grandmother was desperate to get her daughter married. Perhaps she realized only too well that my unworldly grandfather and *mama*s would not take *Ma*'s responsibility seriously. *Ma* who had rejected marriage proposals with top lawyers and police-inspectors, accepted gladly the proposal of an assistant teacher in a small town tucked away deep in south Bihar (now Jharkhand).

Baba's humble schoolteacher's salary had to maintain not just his own family but also a niece and widowed sister.

It was again truly remarkable that *Baba* should understand *Ma*'s thirst for knowledge. He bought textbooks to teach her English. Unfortunately, we three brothers and sisters were born in quick succession. Frequent childbirth put an end to *Ma*'s English lessons. Anyway, *Baba* subscribed to the weekly *Desh*[9] for *Ma*. He brought her library books from the Bengali Club. *Ma*'s book-reading habit was greatly ridiculed by an aunt and father's relatives. But reading gave my mother a space to breathe in order to escape mundane domesticity—and so she could ignore their taunts. Besides, *Ma* had a good flair for writing. Before her marriage, *Ma* had won the second prize in a Bengali short story competition. She wrote stories for Bengali magazines like *Dipali* and *Chitra*.[10] After marriage, *Ma* began writing a novel for the popular Bengali monthly *Basumati*.[11] The stories were simple but I remember she created strong female characters. *Ma* carved out her own space in a life choking with housework. Those times were difficult because there was not much money. We were a large family of six school-going children. Except for a part-time domestic, she had no other help. But *Ma* was especially careful to see that her daughters' studies were not interrupted. Except for light chores she made sure that housework did not encroach on our study time.

We were so used to the daily luxury of delicious meals that we thought nothing about *Ma*'s troubles. Thinking of my selfish behaviour, I am stricken with shame till this day. Every evening we came back from school ravenously hungry. *Ma* would be in the kitchen most of the time. During winter, a long season in Hazaribagh, she would walk across to a cousin's house a few blocks away with a basket of peas. This was her usual beat. She always managed to rush home before we arrived. Once in a while if she was not present in the kitchen when we returned, we would furiously stamp our way to *Khurima*'s house. Poor *Ma* would quickly collect the peas she had shelled and rush back with a guilty expression. While she prepared the evening snack we complained loudly about being terribly hungry. At times *Ma*'s patience snapped, and she would angrily retort, 'I am not your maidservant!' I do not recall *Baba* complaining. On the contrary, overhearing our tantrums one day, he scolded us for being selfish.

Ma made excellent *boris* at home. She turned out delicious milk-based sweets with professional skill. She made mouth-watering salty snacks like *singhara, kachuri, dalpuris* with a variety of stuffings. All this consumed most of her time. But one thing is certain—*Ma* did not become a household drudge. She had a good voice and loved to sing. I remember her humming while cutting vegetables with the *bonti*. She would sing making the beds and hand mix the *dal* to the right consistency for the *bori*. When she cooked on the coal stove, there was a book in her hand. While one hand stirred the ladle, the other would be busy turning over the book's pages. These were *Ma*'s ways to carve out time fo herself, create a private space, in her efforts to reach for the sky.

I realize today that what I am is entirely my mother's handiwork. Father lost his parents and was brought up in his maternal uncle's house. His uncle was no doubt a large-hearted man but extremely conservative about women's education. His own father, that is, *Baba*'s maternal grandfather, sent all his daughters to school. My grandmother and grandaunts were literate, though they were married off in their early teens. But none of my father's cousins, except one, completed school.

By the time our family doctors gave me permission to join school, the Carmelite nuns had set up a convent. The local Bengali girls' school did not have a bus. And though the Government Girls' School did, it was situated at a great distance. I continued to study at home. When *Ma* heard about the new convent school having a bus, she prevailed on *Baba* to admit us there. With admirable courage, *Ma* faced the vicious taunts from her in-laws about making her daughters into *memsahibs*. After schooling, came the ordeal of college. In 1956, Hazaribagh had a single co-educational college. Many of my schoolmates gave up education, as their parents did not approve of co-education. Father's uncle was opposed to the idea of *Baba* sending me to college. *Baba*, who had tremendous respect for his uncle, was in a dilemma. It was *Ma* who persuaded him to send me to college. Once again, she braved the taunts about her daughters getting out of hand.

After that, war was declared. For my postgraduate studies, I had to leave the safe cocoon of our home. My destination was Kolkata. Father's relatives rose up in arms. *Baba* was summoned to an emergency meeting called by his family. He was warned that girls studying at the university were not virgins. One of *Baba*'s cousins even pointed out that if I was already smart, going to a big city would surely make me more brazen. Examples were cited of local girls studying for postgraduation in private. All this brainwashing made my father dither. It was the command of many against one. In this entire hullabaloo, *Ma* stood her ground. After-wards, she was tormented by her cousin sisters-in-law. They made my mother cry with their hurtful insinuations, but could not reverse her decision. *Ma* had a reputation for being stubborn and she showed that her stubbornness could be put to very good use.

Kolkata city opened new doors for me. My thinking underwent a radical change. The climate of political awareness amongst students, their relaxed interaction with female students, was a welcome change from the indecent behaviour girls encountered from men in a small town like Hazaribagh. The vast university library, brilliant visiting lecturers, widened my horizons. Life seemed too perfect. Sadly, this idyllic situation abruptly ended during one summer holiday when *Baba* suffered a massive stroke. I returned home. Our relatives advised *Ma* against sending me back to complete my studies but instead to get a job in Hazaribagh town. Once more, she firmly stood her ground.

She sold off her gold ornaments to help us brothers and sisters to continue with our education. When I decided to get married outside our caste, she ignored her maternal uncle-in-law's stern diktat that the family would boycott our marriage. Assisted by a loyal family friend, *Ma* managed to bring our ailing father from Hazaribagh to the railway station 42 miles away, and after that to Kolkata! As threatened, we were boycotted for many years by Father's maternal relatives. It was only after *Baba*'s death, that the embargo was lifted.

I saw Ritwik Ghatak's[12] *Meghe Dhaka Tara* recently, and realized with a shock that I too would have been doomed like the film's heroine Nita had *Ma* not consented to my marriage. My brothers, a selfish lot, had accused me of having no family consideration. Not for a day did *Ma* succumb to their accusations.

When she faced days of acute financial hardship, *Ma* handled her troubles with dignity and courage. She never turned to relatives for monetary help. She taught me to value money, pointing out the difference between thrift and miserliness, or how to rise above one's circumstances and share or care. *Ma* rose above her lower middle-class existence with a vision of life that she passed on to her daughters. She never talked of getting us married, never hoarded gold ornaments for our marriage. She did not discriminate between her sons and daughters. It is from *Ma* that we learnt to keep our chins up.

Like any of us, *Ma* too had her shortcomings. But her positive qualities far outnumbered these human failings. Perhaps, I would have enjoyed only a conventional relationship—that of a married daughter—with *Ma*, had I not joined the Women's movement. During a life-threatening heart surgery, *Ma* moved in with us—managing my household, nursing me. She was always there when I needed her. Looking back, I realize how remarkably different *Ma* was from the average Bengali mother. I owe this realization to the Women's movement, which made me reflect on my mother's true worth and see her in the correct perspective.

If *Ma* was here today I would say to her:

> *Ma* I am sorry we took your sacrifices, your support for granted. You filled music in my ears with your sweet singing, you inspired me to read Bengali literature, you taught me to care for others. And it was you who shaped my temperament to join the movement. Where would I be if you were not there, *Ma*?

This is not only one daughter's emotional tribute to her mother but a tribute to all the mothers who give up their todays to create better tomorrows for us.

Notes

1. Jamini Roy (1887–1972) was born in Bankura district in West Bengal. He pioneered a highly individualistic art form based on the stylization of the Bengali folk painting tradition.
2. Meera Mukherjee (1923–98) was one of India's most distinguished metal sculptors who created her own art tradition through an intuitive interpretation of the lost wax tradition of the Ghoruas (tribal metal sculptors) of Bastar, Madhya Pradesh.
3. Ishwar Chandra Vidyasagar (1820–91) pioneered widow remarriage and womens' education in 19th century Bengal. He was instrumental in getting the Widow Remarriage Bill enacted by the British in 1856. The first widow remarriage was undertaken in 1870.
4. Goddess Durga was created to destroy evil. Durga was originally worshipped by Ravana the 10-headed demon king who had abducted Rama's wife Sita. In Bengal, the Durga festival and worship in autumn is the largest religio-social festival.
5. Ganesh, the Hindu elephant-headed God is the son of Goddess Durga who has to be worshipped before all other gods and goddesses for success and prosperity. Kartik is the younger son of Goddess Durga whose mount is the peacock. He is the God of War.

6. Ramakrishna Paramhansa (1836–86) is Bengal's most revered saint after Sri Chaitanya. Born in the village of Kamarpukur in Hugli district, to a poor Brahmin family as Gadadhar, he was later christened, Ramakrishna Paramhansadev. He was a great devotee of the Goddess Kali.

7. Ramprasad Sen (1720–81) belonged to Halisahar near Naihati in West Bengal. He was a great devotee of Goddess Kali and composed a large body of songs based on Bengali folk tunes. These were called *Shyamasangeet*. In these songs, which are like odes, he addressed Kali not as a goddess but as a man addressing his mother.

8. Henri Cartier Bresson (1908–2004) was one of the most influential photographers of the 20th century. When asked about the subject of his photograph, he used the expression of capturing 'the defining moment'.

9. *Desh*, a reputed Bengali literary magazine from the Ananda Bazaar Group, first published in 1932.

10. *Dipali* and *Chitra*, Bengali film magazines published in the 1930s.

11. *Basumati*, a renowned Bengali family weekly.

12. Ritwik Ghatak, well-known Bengali film director who created masterpieces like *Ajantrik, Subarnarekha, Meghe Dhaka Tara*.

When Alamelu Shrugged

❧❧

C.S. Lakshmi

Mother, your personality contains the fragrance
of auspicious music.

—Kalidasa

Alamelu, my mother, is a small-built woman. But from her childhood, heavy burdens were placed on her shoulders. They defined her, restricted her and made demands on her as a woman. But every now and then Alamelu shrugged her frail shoulders and let the burdens roll down them, making place for some happy burdens she liked to carry, like educating her daughters and making her children live their life according to their desires and not according to what was expected of them. Every time Alamelu shrugged her shoulders, she changed the order of things at home and created a new power balance. At this point in my life it feels good to be writing about her for she turned ninety on 15 March 2005. She still stitches her blouses and petticoats in her old Singer sewing machine, discusses national politics with enthusiasm and eagerly watches some Tamil serials and politely refuses to come over the phone when I call her at that time. She also has other ways of keeping us out when she so wishes. She wears hearing aids as she has become hard of hearing. Whenever we begin to tell her things that she does not agree with or does not like to hear, I watch her closely. She raises her hand gently and switches off her hearing aid! When I teased her about it once she said she does it to save on battery! That is Alamelu in a nutshell—a woman who does what her heart tells her.

Songs on the Terrace and Cakes with Green and Pink Icing

Alamelu was born in 1915, the eldest in a family of 10 children. She was sent to school and enjoyed her studies but could not continue after the seventh or eighth standard. She got married at the age of eleven to a young man who was twenty. The story goes that my paternal grandmother was ill and that she told father to marry the girl selected by her for him. The girl selected was Alamelu whose aunt had married Father's eldest brother. It seems Father was not very happy with the choice and that he grumbled that he did not want to marry 'that girl with motor-car eyes'. My mother has very large, beautiful eyes, but they do jut out of her face. Hence Father's comments. My Grandmother did some emotional blackmail. She told Father she wanted to see him happily married before she died. Father complied. My grandmother lived for a long time after that. But I don't think Father regretted marrying the girl with 'motor-car eyes'. She made a wonderful life-partner when she came to his house at the age of fifteen, after she came of age.

Alamelu was the eldest child in a large family where along with her own siblings, there were cousins and an older aunt and a grandmother. Her father was a connoisseur of music and Alamelu had been trained well in music. She had a resonant voice and could also play the *veena*. She often talks about nights on the terrace of her house when her father used to ask her to sing with her sisters. People in the neighbourhood waited for this informal concert and sometimes there would be demands from the neighbours for a specific Raga or a song. Her marital household was entirely different. Her mother-in-law was a widow who had single handedly brought up her five sons and two daughters. She had tonsured her head when her husband had died and she held some strong views about what a woman could and could not do. One thing that she was definite about was that a decent woman could not sing and entertain her husband. Occasionally, Alamelu played the *veena* at night when she was with her husband not because he knew anything about music but because he did not mind her playing. Her mother-in-law put an end to that because she used to sleep right outside their bedroom door and knew what was going on inside. However, her mother-in-law was not exactly a cruel woman. Alamelu had long hair that came down to her waist and her mother-in-law helped her wash her hair and she also patiently taught her how to cook. All the same, when they came to live in Chennai for a while, Alamelu did enjoy the freedom. It was not that they went out much. But Alamelu spent a lot of time playing the *veena*. She longed to go for music concerts that had become a regular affair in Chennai, but her husband was not too keen. She wrote about her life in a small journal that she has given me. In that she says that there was a music hall nearby and that she stood on the verandah of her house to listen to the music concert going on nearby. Just like her childhood years, there was an old gentleman nearby who often came when she began to play the *veena*. Once, when Father returned from the office, mother was playing the *veena* and father did not quite like it. He told her that he would not like her to play for others. Mother cut off the strings of her *veena* and did not play the *veena* for a long time. She began to play only when she started teaching my sister and me. But she was not one to mourn her lot and become inactive.

Father was a voracious reader and he taught her English and she taught him Tamil for he had studied in the Malayalam medium. Popular Tamil magazines came home and all the serials were bound and kept. As a child growing up in Mumbai, I remember Mother taking my younger brother and me to a tailoring class run by a Parsi lady. I minded my younger brother while she took her lessons. Until I left home at the age of nineteen, I only wore clothes stitched by Mother. Her enthusiasm to learn things never seemed to abate. Much later, when she was in her late 50s or so, Mother joined a baking course. She wrote out the recipes in English, which Father cor-rected after she came home. She passed the course with flying colours. When I next went home, Mother baked a cake for me secretly. She and Father had come to the station to see me off. At the station, Mother took the cake out of the box. It was a small round cake with green and pink icing and Mother proudly gave it to me saying, 'Eat it in the train.' I heard Father grumbling, 'Is there anything left for me?' and Mother reassured him that there was another one at home for him.

Food as Communication, Food as Adventure

That cake with green and pink icing was not the only adventure Alamelu had with food. Looking back, I feel that food was not just a preoccupation with women like Alamelu. There was a way in which she turned food into a mode of communication, assertion and adventure. For many years, I associated different seasons with different items of food and intertwined with them were memories of procuring, preparation and consumption and the effect each one had on your stomach and physical system. The months preceding April were months meant for pickling, especially tender mango pickle and *avakkai* and for making jackfruit jam and raw jackfruit chips. The entire process of cutting open the jackfruit and taking the fruit out with oil-smeared hands, slicing the fruit for jam, setting aside some for daily eating—dipping the fruit into honey and eating it was the most delicious way—and while making raw fruit chips, the entire house would be filled with the smell of smoking coconut oil and melting jaggery. The jackfruit jam would be used over the following months for puddings and snacks in which the jackfruit jam would be coated with rice dough and steamed, wrapped in a banana leaf.

In the summer holidays, we would be entrusted with a variety of duties. One of us would accompany mother to the main wholesale market to buy a basket of *malgova* mangoes, a special variety, and a basket of mangoes from Salem and half a basket of *badami* mangoes. No one ever refused to accompany Mother, for the child who accompanied her always got to taste the mangoes the wholesale vendors offered. There was also the additional bonus of a ride back in a horse-drawn cart we called *jutka*, in Bangalore. Mother would spend some time looking for a *jutka* with a healthy horse. The moment she sat in it she would tell the *jutka* driver that she would get down if he beat or poked the horse. The summer months were also months meant for making rice crispies called *vadam* to be preserved in huge tins for a whole year. The *vadam*-making activity would start early in the morning and by eleven, Mother would have pressed the cooked and steamed rice dough through various moulds on to a white *veshti* spread out in the backyard. Mother used to wear a hat to protect herself from the sun and on a summer day if she began looking for the hat, we instinctively knew what was to follow.

The monsoon and winter months meant sesame seed and peanut jaggery balls, besides all the festival eating. We also knew what to expect in terms of food when we fell sick. The sick child got properly pampered. Apart from herbal decoctions and various poultices, there were other 'specials' for the sick child. The silver bowl in which all of us ate till we began to eat off plates, would be brought out. Two large servings of hot rice would be put in it, a spoon of homemade *ghee* poured on it and then with the bottom of a thick, rounded spoon the rice was mashed so that the child would not have to make an effort to chew it. The clear, top layer of *rasam* with pepper and cumin seed powder in it, just seasoned with mustard in pure *ghee*, was added and mixed with the rice. After this, a roasted *pappad* was placed next to the silver bowl. The silver bowl along with a spoon was brought to the bedside of the child and placed on the small wooden stool that was used to press rice noodles. (This was an all-purpose stool that we also used on the days we had oil baths, to sit on, waiting for mother to rub oil warmed with cumin seed, pepper and rice, into our hair.) The fragrance of *ghee* and *rasam* would already have wafted to where the child lay and with the gleaming silver bowl before it, no child could resist eating what was given. A child below 10 may be told a story after that. A smaller child would drift into sleep listening to a soft lullaby sung in Raga Neelambari. Mother could bring magic to her resonant voice when she was in the mood.

A few years ago, I persuaded Mother to write a journal. The journal had several references to food. What she wrote had to do with producing food during the most difficult of occasions. Like in wartime, when she walked up and down flights of stairs with heavy bags of wheat, to knock at the doors of some friendly Punjabi neighbours who were willing to give rice in exchange. Like the time she visited Hardwar in 1932, before all of us were born, when the whole family was stranded at the station waiting for a train delayed by several hours. Mother remembered seeing a woman in one of the huts nearby. She wandered around looking for her, found her and requested her to cook a lot of rice. Meanwhile, Mother went and bought a huge basket, some leaves and earthen pots of curds for which Hardwar was famous at that time. She came back and the rice was ready. Mother requested the lady to crush on the stone some pungent *chutney*. She covered the basket with the leaves and put rice in it. She added the creamy curds and mixed it with the rice. She packed the *chutney* in a leaf-holder. She paid the lady for her trouble and carried the basket to the station. The family ate it with relish and everyone told her it was like nectar from heaven.

Our household was strictly vegetarian. Even garlic and onions were not used often. But Mother would use a separate stove to make us eggs and opposition was always quelled with the explanation that it was the doctor's advice! Our Alsatian dog at home got its meat separately cooked in the garage. Its name was Lilly. It had strict orders not to enter the kitchen. Lilly would sit with its entire body in the kitchen keeping its hind legs and tail out, pretending that it was not in the kitchen. When I think about it now I feel that women like my mother Alamelu were doing something similar. They were just pretending to comply with the rules of the family and the society, but were simultaneously quietly breaking them.

Mother eats only once a day these days and at night she has a special gruel we call *kanji*. She prepares the gruel powder with all kinds of sprouted grains and adds cardamom and nutmeg to it for flavour. It tastes heavenly. She prepares an extra bottle for all of us but is yet to give us the recipe. Nor has she given me the recipe for *rasam* powder. I ask her for it often.

'What do you need it for? As long as I am alive I will make it for you' is her reply.

I once told her hesitantly, 'But what will I do after your lifetime, *Amma*?'

'What is your elder sister there for?' she retorted.

A Time to Sing and Dance, a Time to Study

Food was only one of the adventures Mother led us into. Since she had not been able to pursue music in the manner she wanted to, she made sure that my sister and I were well trained in music. Had we shown an inclination to pursue it as a career she may have stood by us. One major decision she took was to put me in a dance class at a time when not many girls from middle-class families were learning dance. It was more an upper-class trait. To those who questioned her decision to bring dance into our family, she had the same classic excuse. She said that the doctor had advised dance as an exercise since I was very skinny! She saw to it that I performed on stage and that I had a formal *arangetram*. I don't know how she managed all this with my father's salary, who was an Accounts Officer. And where studies were concerned, we were exempt from any household chores as Mother managed all that with the help of a cook and a maidservant. Our job was to study as much as we wanted as long as we wanted. During exams, I would get up early, at around 2 or 3 A.M., Mother would get up along with me so that I won't feel lonely. Sometimes, she would ask me if I was hungry and I always was. She would go to the kitchen and make some hot *dosai* and bring it. I still remember Mother waiting for me at the Kalasipalayam bus stand in Bangalore late one evening. My graduation ceremony was in Mysore and I was taking a bus from Mysore to Bangalore. I got down from the bus and told Mother that I had got the gold medal in History and two cash prizes. She stood for a moment and looked at me, tears streaming down her face.

I had made up my mind that I would go to Chennai and do my M.A. from Madras Christian College. Father was not at all in favour of this decision. He had already retired and he was working in Kottayam, Kerala, in the Rubber Board. He told me I could do my M.A. in Bangalore. But I wanted to spread my wings. My sister Rajeswari was working in a bank and gave me some money to apply to Madras Christian College. The letter confirming my admission came soon after. And here was Father opposing it. He left the next day. Mother came into my room and asked me, 'Do you think going to Madras will make a difference in your life?' 'Yes,' I replied. She left the room. She went to a bank and took a gold loan pledging her jewels. She went and bought a suitcase and four *saris* for me because I was now a postgraduate student and could not wear half-*saris* anymore. I still remember the colours of those *Khatau* voile *saris*—yellow, blue, pink and a very light purple one with delicate floral prints. When my sister returned from the bank, we were all packed to go the next day. 'You never did this for me,' my sister complained. 'You did not ask for it,' Mother replied.

We took the night train to Chennai, got down at the Central Station the following morning and then went to the Park Station to take the local train to Tambaram. I was sitting next to the window, looking out. As the train neared Tambaram, Mother leaned towards me and whispered in my ear, 'All Lakshmi's dreams are going to come true.' It was a very poignant moment for me and I have always kept it in my heart as a precious moment. Sometime back, when a book of mine was published, I recalled this moment and dedicated the book to Alamelu—my mother, an artist and a dreamer. She was living with me for a while then. When she read it she said, 'Did I say that?' I wanted to tell her that she had said that and so much more. But the words got stuck in my throat.

After that first trip, she was with me when I decided to become a school teacher in a small town in Tamil Nadu. She was there to send me off to Delhi for my Ph.D. When I decided to remain single and much later decided to marry a person of my choice, she stood by me. Not that she agreed with many things I did, but she thought she should uphold my freedom to do what I wanted. And she has been that way always. Sometime back, I told her that SPARROW[1] was suffering from a financial crunch. She took out her chequebook and from her pension money, wrote me a cheque in favour of SPARROW for two thousand rupees.

Singing a Song for Subramaniam

I was not the only child Alamelu gave wings to. When my younger brother wanted to study further, she sold off all her silver vessels to put together some money. And when he decided to marry a Christian girl, Mother went to the church and shook hands with the priest. Later she lived with my brother for 10 years, bringing up his children. When her heart gave her the reasons, she was willing to break any custom or rule doing that shoulder-shrugging act of hers.

My father, C.R. Subramaniam, died of thyroid cancer. Towards the end, he could not speak because they had removed his voice box. He wrote out what he wanted to say. He wrote a note to my mother urging her never to give up her music. Mother keeps that note in her spectacle box. When the hearse came to take his body to the cremation grounds, I decided that I would go with the body. I went, and sat next to the body and in a few minutes, much to the surprise of many people gathered there, Mother was also sitting next to me. The priest tried to tell her that the *Shastra*s did not allow a woman to go to the cremation grounds. Mother wanted to know which *Shastra*s said that. 'I have lived with him for more than 50 years and I have a right to see his body burn,' she said. There was no high drama. Everything happened quietly. A few more women joined and we went to the cremation grounds. As my brother lit the pyre, she began to sing a song which father used to like. '*Sivarama Krishna, Govinda Narahari Narayana Kasi Viswanatha...*' rose her resonant voice with not a tremour. She completed the song, brought her palms together in a salute and turned away.

A year after my father's death, I was in Chennai in connection with my research. I met a wonderful lady called Savithri Rajan, who had learnt *veena* from the famous Veenai Dhanammal. I wrote to mother about it. Mother wrote to me to ask her if she would teach her the *tanam* aspect of Carnatic music that she was never able to learn. Savithri Rajan graciously agreed to teach her. Mother came down and lived with me for three months and took lessons from her, much to the amazement of the rest of the family. Every evening when I came back from my research I used to find her practising. She mastered the *tanam* playing and only then left Chennai. After father's death she had taken to wearing the traditional 9 yards *sari*. It was hot in Chennai and with her sensitive skin she found it very difficult to manage with the heavy *sari*. I told her that she should wear the regular 6 yards, the one she always wore. 'I have entered this locality in a 9 yards *sari*. What will people say?,' she said. 'Are you really going to bother about what these people say, *Amma*?,' I said. When I came back in the evening she had put on one of my 6 yards *saris* and since then has worn only soft-cotton 6 yards *saris*.

Alamelu is generous when it comes to gifts for her great grandchildren. Even Khintu, the little girl who is growing up in my house, gets money and gifts when she visits Mother. I am always telling her stories about Mother because I have so many things around me that she has used. There is the copper pot we used to store water, which has her pet name *Alamu* written in Tamil on the edge of the mouth. There is her *veena* carved in black wood and presented to her by my grandfather. All the deep frying pans she has bought ever since the birth of my elder brother for 8 and 12 *annas* are lying in my little kitchen. There is also the rice noodle stool and the brass press that goes with it. I have removed the press and use it as a stool. In fact, a visitor from abroad looked at it and asked me hesitantly if it was a traditional toilet for children! With the stool also came the iron-pounder which mother had used to put pressure on the press. Wrapped in a newspaper, it lies behind my bedroom door ready to be used if a thief ever dares to sneak into my house. All her other cooking vessels are also with me for she could not throw them away. People joke that all these are Alamelu's bequest to me.

Last year or so Mother got tempted by the watch ads in the media. She told my brother that she needed a new watch. He told her that she really did not need it as she did not go out much, besides, her eyes were weak and she could not see the time any more. Mother went to the market quietly and got herself a Ritter watch. She showed it to me the other day.

Occasionally, when she goes out to the temple she wears it. She asked me if I would like to have it. I told her I did not need it. But it is possible she may bequeath it to me along with all the cuttings she has made of home medicines, *rangoli*s and recipes, and her various music notes. She knows I won't throw them away. For her, they are not objects but memories she would like to keep for herself and for others to keep. All her things lying in various places in my little house spread her warmth around me. Often, I stand by the kitchen window where I have placed the copper pot and run my fingers over her name etched on the pot. During those moments Alamelu seems eternal.

Note

1. SPARROW (Sound and Picture Archives for Research on Women).

An Outsider at Home

Neela Bhagwat

I see you at times in
my sister, or my friend,
sometimes in my child
and at times in my lover.
—Neela Bhagwat

The relationship between a mother and her child is unalterable and, therefore, unique. So is the relationship of a child with its father. Many of us frequently take our parents for granted. Mothers are taken for granted a great deal more than fathers. Except, I think, amongst the economically-depressed classes. And yet, there is a difference in their approach to the child.

Had I thought of my mother in a similar way? I am not certain. A proud individual, my mother would not have tolerated being taken for granted. Besides, she was too devoted a mother to allow her children to suffer. The first of these two traits, pride, is commonly found among *Chitpavan* Brahmins, which was my mother's caste. But her devotion to her children was entirely characteristic of her—it was ingrained in her identity. My parents related to us as one indivisible 'unit'. And yet, let me add, Mother's devotion to us, her children, was difficult to match. I remember the many occasions when Father was summoned to run errands for us—rushing to examination halls or railway stations. Despite his busy schedule he did whatever Mother wanted him to do for us.

It was difficult for us as children to understand the texture of our parents' relationship. However, one thing was certain, Father was our link with the outside world and Mother was the family authority with regard to small household matters. Father seemed to me an ideal individual—indeed, the ideal man. And Mother was someone who never erred—nor could she be ever questioned. A woman, who although spent most of her time in the kitchen was in fact, also supporting activities outside the threshold for the rest of the family ....

Yes, I was acutely aware of these wide distinctions. But neither the kitchen nor an influential position appealed to me. I always believed that the kitchen and authority were things one had to take charge of when the need arose and were to be given up once the task was accomplished.

My mother sensed this discomfort and worried about me. Whenever she expressed her anxiety, I asked:

> What is so great about family life? Tell me, what does one exactly do in a family? One gets up, picks up the vessels, messes them by cooking. Then one cleans them, places them back on the shelf; the outcome of this entire activity is food, which one finishes in exactly half an hour. If this is what you mean by family and married life I have no interest in it.

When I think of this statement in today's context, I am aware of the perpetual conflict between creativity and the management of day-to-day existence. By creativity, I mean the process of developing certain basic responses to emotions, sensations and abstract ideas. A child shows her/his talent in the nature of its response to its environment. Development of talent depends primarily on the socialization provided by parents and also on the child's response to it.

As a child, I was encouraged to pursue intellectual goals. But my sentimental and romantic moods remained un-nurtured. I was of course, dissuaded from learning *Kathak* dance, which was truly my first love. Learning music was considered socially-less hazardous. It did not involve physical proximity with the opposite sex. Moreover, our family had a musical tradition. Mother used to play the violin, Father sang.

Our aunts took part in the *Rashtriya Melas*. It was expected that I would learn to sing and my brother would learn the *tabla*.

A major choice in life was to some extent imposed on me. I interpret this as a conflict between the traditional approach to one's own body [or choices?] and a more individualistic or modern approach to it. Many years later, when I was married to Arun Khopkar, I encountered a similar conflict. I had to choose between theatre and music. I was forced to choose music. I wanted to postpone making a choice. Perhaps, left to myself I would have chosen music. Anyway, on both these occasions, I accepted the choice that had been imposed upon me and that was how I became a professional music artist. The idea of asserting myself in the realm of music is perhaps reflected when I write my own compositions. Music left the doors open to lived experience and enabled their expression through a musical composition. The traditional form of *Khayal* music can often become a vehicle for modern feminist ideas. When two of my compositions, speaking of the joy of being independent and the need for friends to come together, appeared on a compact disc in London, I was truly happy. I say happy, because I could use my art form to convey ideas about life.

This is the philosophical and artistic aspect regarding the choice of my art form. In practice, my decision to join a music school was supported by my mother. My father was more keen that I pursue an academic career. But Mother said, 'Let her learn now. It may be difficult after marriage.' This brings to mind the question she asked me when I went to meet her the very next morning after my first marriage on 26 May 1967. 'Where are your clothes Neela?' Mother asked me, 'you haven't brought them for me to wash?' I was almost in tears. How these small things matter in intimate relationships! After marriage, I had a house to myself for four years. During this period, I always returned to my mother's house when I was ill. I never sat down to clean the grain, or get the flour ground for *chapatis*. Mother did all that for me. I never purchased expensive party *saris* for myself. I borrowed them from her. I had no time, nor desire to work for economic stability in life. I was busy acquainting myself with dance, theatre, cinema, painting; and meeting various artistes, trying to know them as individuals. My grounding as an artiste happened during this time. My companionship with Arun was extremely creative in this respect.

Arun joined the Film and Television Institute of India (FTII) in Pune and I was left alone. By then, we had lost our temporary accommodation. I returned to my parents' house in December 1971 and I have lived with them ever since.

In 1976, we decided to have a child. Till then, I could not think of a child as I was not confident that I could provide the kind of nurturing that I had received. My mother believed I was one of those women who would sacrifice their personal aspirations and dreams to pursue a higher ambition. It is true that during these years I was deeply involved in the progressive political and socio-cultural movement and never aligned with the establishment. Mother and many others, thought that a person of my temperament could not and perhaps, should not aspire for motherhood. And there I was, discussing with her what could be done if I had a child. I hoped that the child would be brought up the way I was. By then, I had admitted to my mother that my marriage might not survive. Yet, I wanted a child.

That was when I made the most important request to my mother. She assured me, 'Yes, I'll look after your baby for two years.'

Her words gave me courage to explore motherhood. In August 1977, I delivered my son—Tappa or Tapan, as we call him. In July 1978, Arun and I separated. We decided to remain friends. Initially, Mother was opposed to the idea of our remaining friends, despite the separation, but soon she understood the need for it. I explained to her how important it was for the child to be in touch with his roots. She responded positively.

I married Nandu Dhaneshwar in June 1983. My mother was very apprehensive about our relationship since Nandu was 9 years younger to me. My son, Tappa, on the other hand, was happy. He said to me: 'Nana, two of us were so lonely! It is nice that Nandu will be here with us!'

His positive response created a perfect setting for my relationship with Nandu. There were gaps and yet, a very strong bond has developed between us. There were fights and conflicts and Tapan often commented: 'Do what you want when I am not there but don't turn me into a *Sunday Observer* (a Sunday paper).' Sometimes he asked: 'Why is it that when the grandparents quarrel, I have a hearty laugh and when you and Nandu fight, I feel insecure?,' 'You needn't feel insecure darling! We don't fight, we only discuss certain details and that is an essential part of life. Don't I discuss so many things with you?' I tried to reassure him. Tapan would not give up his arguments easily.

Life goes on and one's responses change. The only continuity is the devotion to the child in my soul. I extend this feeling to my students, who learn music from me and to my young accompanists, Girish and Milind. And to many other friends, both women and men, with whom I bond. My mother and I have arguments regarding trivial matters in the house. There is tension but we forget it when something more important appears on the scene. We share our worries and anxieties as well as joys and happy moments in bringing up my son. Nandu does not interfere and my father joins in only when the need arises.

I don't know what kind of a mother I am. But I would not have been what I am, had I denied myself the experience of motherhood. Whenever I reflect on questions of motherhood, I remember Arun's mother and how marvellous she was. It is difficult to forget her warmth. And I think of my sister-in-law Shobha Bhagwat, my sister Vasanti (Dr Leena Mohadikar) and friends Anjali Monteiro and Sushama Deshpande who are blessed with wonderful motherhood. Our collective experiences have been composed in Raga Durga by me. Traditionally, one finds songs in this Raga in praise of the Mother Goddess, Durga. But I have expressed my song of motherhood in Raga Durga ....

Tum hi ho adhar mayi
Daras det paras karat
Karuna hi teri reet
Kabhi tum ho bahena kabhi sakhi pyari
Kabhi balak ho bilkhat
Kabhi piya ki reet nyari

(Motherhood is the
basis of all relationships,
You, who are ever tangible,
I see you at times in
my sister, or my friend,
sometimes in my child
and at times in my lover.)

Her Infinite Variety

❧❧

Roshan G. Shahani

When my mother turned ninety-one, we had a birthday party for her.
As we sang 'Happy Birthday' to her, she joined in the singing and clapping. And the air was filled with laughter as all of us felt, however briefly,
a sense of gaiety—her daughters, son-in-law, grandchildren, nieces and
nephews. My mother had become a child once more, we would talk to
her and treat her tenderly and maternally as I had with my children long
ago. She had reached that twilight region, where I could no longer reach
out to her, no longer communicate with her, except as with an infant—
cajoling her, chiding her, singing to her, holding her in my arms. But
that is not how I want to remember my mother, helpless and childlike.
I would like to remember my mother, the way she was, before her lapse
into oblivion. Perhaps the very act of writing helps exorcise the sad ghosts
that haunt us. There is also the hope that it might make her whole again,
so broken was she in mind, body and spirit.

Yet, to document her life, is to fix her, frozen and immobile, like a face
in a studio photograph. There are so many ambiguities, so many memories and associations, her letters, diaries, jottings, her way of speaking
teaching, her infinite variety, that no photograph could capture, no family
tree contain. Then how can *I* begin, so enmeshed as I have been in my
mother's life? Can I say my mother was thus and thus? So many threads

so many patches—the quilt can never be complete. Besides, can this recourse to a cliché-ridden metaphor, threadbare with overuse, stitch
together the variegated pieces that went into the making of a mother's
life? It is at the time of writing and of recall, that I realize how a seemingly
ordinary life becomes elusive and complex in its telling. It is also, at
moments like these, that I regret not having 'listened' more carefully to
the inner rhythms of my mother's life, of her relationships, or attempted
to 'understand' the tales she had to tell.

Fragments come wafting one's way—fragments of fragments, memories
of memories—so that you can no longer sift the real from the imagined.
My mother was one of eight children, four of whom were her half-brothers.
Characteristically, this fact was never revealed to me. Brought up on fairy
tales of monstrous stepbrothers and stepmothers, I as the youngest of
three, needed to be protected from what my parents must have thought
were harsh truths. There was a *mama* who left for Burma, never to return—
his letters could make a history of its own. I came across one when I was
clearing our sad house after my mother's death. He was taken by the
Japanese for a British spy and tortured to the point of death ... there was
another *mama* who would call my mother '*dantadi*' on account of her
buck teeth, yet another, who would plait her hair, another who disapproved
of my mother's seven-year courtship with my father. All her brothers
totally disapproved of my mother's desire and determination to join
college. 'Who will cook and clean?', was the general grouse.

Strangely enough, my grandparents were not totally averse to my
mother's desire for education. Perhaps, it was not so strange after all.
My grandfather was an educated man, a postmaster by profession, who,
I believe, spoke impeccable English and hence, had been appointed
by his rich relatives—the K. Wadia family of jewellers to attend to
their largely British clientele. It was, I am sure, the kind of old-world
English, that might sound pompous to a post-colonial generation, but
which must have then seemed very impressive. My mother was wont
to recall this man's sense of dignity, a dignity that might have been sorely
tested in the hey-day of British rule. She would relate a particular incident that has long been ingrained in my memory. Once, a Britisher
jumped the queue at the post office as my grandfather sat on the other
side of the office window. The *sahib* did it as a matter of course, expecting
to be served before the natives. He was taken aback when he was told
politely, but firmly by my grandfather to await his turn. 'So did he go

back?', I would ask my mother anxiously, 'Of course. He *had* to', was my mother's reply. Did this actually happen? Did my mother really tell me this story? Or is it my imagination playing tricks on me? My mother's fancy? Or of the old man I never saw? As in the game of Chinese Whispers, so many tales get retold in each telling that they get transformed into family myths. Yet, that is how we like to cherish them, build our own family tree. For they were our ancestors, people who gave us a place to stand on.

My mother got further support from my father to complete her education. She had first met him when she was still at school, the Pandey School, to which my mother owed lasting loyalty. My father was her English and French teacher. Given my father's temperament, it must have been a lively, even tempestuous relationship, but a tender one as well. He was a stern, unbending man and her schoolmaster, but he appreciated pluck and intelligence, both of which my mother had in plenty. They would both recall the time when my father had given the class an essay to write, 'Is Poverty an Evil?' Since, it was a hypothetical and not a rhetorical question, and since my mother had an independent mind, she asserted in the manner of Bernard Shaw that poverty was the greatest of crimes and the worst of evils. My father, who must have expected a more conventional and romantic response—the poor-but-happy syndrome, reprimanded her for her unorthodox views. My mother, however, argued her way through, as she did in all the subsequent years that I knew them as parents. My father would get extremely annoyed at being contradicted, yet he would respect her for that very daring. Had she been a more pliable woman, my father would have trampled all over her and held her in contempt for it. That did not happen. My father would jokingly call my mother his Pygmalion, implying that as her teacher, she was *his* creation, one that he had come to love. My mother, not to be outdone, would tell him with matching wit, that she was nobody's creation but her own!

If my memory serves me well, my mother was one among seven girls to have graduated from Wilson College and then in 1926, she and her sister went to Nagpur where my mother had got a teaching job. Today, when I look back, I think it was rather unusual for two young women to be allowed to stay on their own in the 1920s. I appreciate my grandmother's enlightened spirit and pragmatic views that allowed this independence to her two daughters. I am not very surprised, however, because

Mai had always been very progressive in her ways. Possibly, the very liberal tradition in which we grew up, could be attributed, partially at least, to this firm old lady. She was not very pious; she did not ritualize religion, she did not even cover her head, at least not at home, either with a *sari* or a *mathu banoo*. In fact, the kind of taboos imposed on girls even of my generation, were not inflicted on either her daughters or her daughters-in-law. What is more, unlike one of the *mama*s, *Mai* did not object to the long 7-year-old courtship of my parents and to my father's regular visits to the Gimi household. In fact, when my paternal grandfather raised some trivial objection, she told him gaily '*Jab miya bibi razi/to kya karega kaazi?*' (when man and woman are determined to marry, the *kaazi* has no say in the matter). I can picture his dismay at this unexpected boldness from a woman. My mother must have shocked the arrogant man even further when he had occasion to express his disapproval against her wearing high heels—nobody in his family did so. 'But I do', my mother claims to have said perkily.

I have vague memories of my mother's recollection of her first visit to the Mistri Clan's Andheri Bungalow. No one from the large family emerged from their spacious interiors to welcome her and make her feel at home. This is only a conjecture, but my mum, who rarely visited the suburbs of Bombay, retained the impression that Andheri was a very gloomy place. It could, of course, have been the name that had conjured up the image of darkness; but could it not have been her association with that somber, unfriendly atmosphere of the bungalow?

As a child I was everything that my mother was not. She used to call me *Bikan Sasli* (Timid Rabbit) after the folk tale, in which the rabbit imagines that the heavens have fallen, when actually a berry had plopped onto its head.

So many memories ... and in each one I see myself clinging to my mother. A picnic at Juhu—planes swooping low, I am running along the beach to my mother, hands over my head, lest the plane fall, my mother smiling reassuringly, admonishing my sister and brother, hysterical with laughter .... Yet, another wisp of memory—my first day at school— my mother relinquishing my 4-year-old hand, betraying me to a fearful world.

My mother read me many stories—one that filled me with obsessive fascination was the story of the vain Ariadne who was turned into a spider by the avenging Minerva. I was vain about my long hair. Would I be turned into one? My mother sang songs with me and 'Clemantine' would make me shed tears with the line—'Thou art lost and gone forever.' It was strange that on her deathbed, when to divert her attention, I would sing this familiar song to her, she would tell me plaintively, '*Maney rarvu avech*' (I want to cry)—it wasn't so strange after all. We had interchanged roles and both, in turn, had experienced childlike fears and uncertainties on the one hand, maternal tenderness and understanding, on the other.

Another childhood memory, this time linked with history, was of one bewildering evening. I have fragmented recollections of hurrying home with my *ayah*, Isabel, from our evening outing at Cama Baag (at Grant Road) ... crowded trams ... hurrying up Gowalia Tank ... rushing past the familiar Chakki with its fascinating biscuit-shaped stepping stone ... frightened yet excited, because I was the bearer of terrible news ... panting it out—Gandhiji was dead. And my mother, instead of appreciating me for being her source of information, looking very sombre and very grim. I hated her looking that way ... then my mother tuning in to the radio, inevitably accompanied by me, listening , I think to Nehru's moving valediction—while I felt lost and ignored.

My mother was a staunch admirer of Gandhi and Nehru, whereas, my father, despite feeling the stirrings of nationalism—that he shared with the country in the 1940s—had become disillusioned too soon. There were endless arguments, even battles on the home front over political issues. Although, I sided (silently of course) with my mother, I wished she would not argue. I would compare her unconsciously with other mothers. They were all young and attractive; they wore make-up and Western clothes or *sari*s the more fashionable non-Parsi way. If they visited school, these mothers were reverential to the teachers, whereas my mother, being a teacher herself, would tell them very courteously but very firmly, things that the teachers may not have liked to hear. I would die a thousand deaths each time she visited school. Above all, other mothers cooked and served, they did not read and if they did, they were fashion magazines. They did not read the papers, they did not give talks on the All India Radio, they did not step out into the wide, open world, they were at home when the children returned from school. They held no opinions or strong convictions and that was how I wanted my mother to be. In the quietist, tranquillized 1950s, which coincided with my girlhood, the mom-and-apple-pie image, at least its Indian version, was strongly embedded in me, but my mother would not conform to that image. As a child, whenever my mother scolded me, my mind's eye would conjure up this scene—my father and a beautiful young woman with shoulder-length hair (not an inch longer or shorter), in a white bridal dress, kneeling at the church altar to get married. The woman was cast in the image of someone I used to see around the neighbourhood, the scene was set in St Stephen's Church at Warden Road which I used to frequent with Isabel. My real-life mother was old, plain and clever. She did not fit into this picture frame at all.

A childlike imagination can be charming but innocence preserved too long sours into ignorance. I always remained the little one. But how little was little? At 10, I used to marvel that babies could be born 'just like that' and my mother let me marvel. At sixteen, when the Nanavati case[1] rocked the city, my father declared it should not be discussed in my presence and my mother contradicted him only to add sanctimoniously that I should know the consequences a woman had to pay for marital infidelity. I was eighteen when Mummy and I were discussing *Adam Bede* in an animated fashion. That of course none could take away from us—literature remained a common bond that nothing could sever. Then I happened to mention Hetty Sorrel's illegitimate baby. All of a sudden the animation faded, my mother looked embarrassed and I flushed with guilt.

My sister used to advise Daddy jokingly to lock me up in a glass showcase—needless to say I was not amused. In so many ways—in matters of education, careers, travels, religion—my parents were progressive but in matters regarding sex, birth, death, boyfriends, dates and crushes there was a Victorian prudery that cramped me. A certain refinement dropped like a decorous veil, hiding us in our own silence. My father's primness, although contradictorily, he was in many ways an unconventional man—coupled with the 39-year-old age difference between my mother and me, were the contributory factors. Then there was my own reticence, but this was at least partially, the consequence and not the cause of the barrier. The rebelliousness I experienced has long since faded but it remained long enough to make me vow that I would not let this difference separate me from my children. Did I succeed? Only they can tell! These recollections are now touched with amusement but they are also shadowed by regret. My mother and I were never foes. I wish we could have been friends.

Even while I tried to slough-off certain facets of my mother, I identified with her in many ways. I played at 'Teacher-Teacher' ever since I began to play. My mother was a born teacher and could bring things to life as few teachers could. In a sense, she was my last teacher as well— her own helplessness and dependence taught me patience and endurance and capability, which I did not know I possessed.

What used to amuse Mum, even exasperate her, would be my insistence that she improve my style of writing English. I learnt from her that 'Nice' was not a nice adjective. She fired my imagination. Trees were greener and kings 'kinglier', storms stormier, when my mother evoked them. Akbar's greatness, Ashoka's wisdom, Jhansi ki Rani's valour—all were magnified in my imagination because it was she who had re-enacted their grandeur, their wisdom, their valour. 'God blew with his winds and they were scattered,' Elizabeth I was supposed to have uttered this triumphant cry when the English defeated the Spanish Armada. But the way my mother would proclaim these words, it would seem as though she had voiced the triumphant cry of glory. With her I would then ride the crest of victory. We would share Wordsworth's rapture at the sight of the daffodils, we would feel the Ancient Mariner's loneliness, lost at sea. However, burdened with loads of homework, packing of school bags and books, maths practise that I could never grasp with or without tears, there were times when I would want to check her rhetorical flow. However, years later, when as a college student I told her that she was the best teacher I have ever had, I remember her face all aglow.

My mother's love for literature remained with her till the end of her days. Among the poems she would quote, would be the haunting lines from *The Rime of the Ancient Mariner*,

Alone, alone, all all alone, alone on a wide, wide sea ....

Could she have been speaking of her own solitary condition, the solitude of the old and the dying? Or must it be an older sorrow, lost in time? It was after she was gone that I came across a little red diary, recording various tuition turns in the year 1969. In the midst of those matter-of-fact entries, I came upon one marked against the third of October. She had quoted here these poignant lines that haunt me still ... that was the day my father had died.

I shared with my mother the melancholy and the mellowness of the year that followed my father's agonizing death. For her, it was like an Indian Summer, sad yet, serene. She picked up the threads of life, resumed her teaching a couple of days after his death, took on his insurance work. I found she was treating me more as an adult, took greater interest in my friends than before. She had never ever neglected us, but her life had centred around my father. Her intellectual pursuits continued. She abridged old classics, worked on translation projects, and attended talks and lectures.

When I was working on the first draft of this book, I would sit at my mother's secretaire in our old house, which was still with us at the time. I would get a queer feeling of *deja vu*. Was I mutating into my own mother, bending over the desk, as she used to, with papers scattered before me, spectacles on my nose, asking my husband and children for suggestions, complaining of a stiff neck and an aching back at the end of it all? I regret I had not taken a keener interest in her work at the time, but I should not be too hard on myself. I had my own young life to lead. But today, every piece of paper, every remnant of a life gone by, cries out for salvation. It is the lives of the dead that haunt us, not those of the living.

Among the various pursuits that my mother now had time for was, embroidery. As a finishing touch to the variegated flowers that she had embroidered on a satin quilt for my sister-in-law, she had wanted to stitch in these lines:

Age cannot wither her
Nor custom stale
Her infinite variety

I quote these lines here, not only because of the infinite variety of my mother's life, but because of the varied relationships she shared with a diverse lot of people—her grandchildren, daughter-in-law, sister, sisters-in-law. But there is a deep bond that my mother shared with a person so unlike her that I felt I *had* to write about it, especially since I have had reservations about female bonding and women's support systems.

When I got married, my major anxiety had been regarding how my mother and mother-in-law would take to each other. In every way the two women have been poles apart. My mother exuded confidence, inspired awe, even terror. She loved good clothes and fine jewellery, even after she was widowed. Her silver-grey hair would always be rinsed, waved and set. Even when she had to have her passport photograph taken, she would get her hair done beforehand at the beauty parlour. She would wear embroidered *saris* with perfectly matching lace blouses; a delicate bracelet, a small handbag, an exquisite *sari*-pin and dainty high-heeled shoes completed the ensemble. Our house was always neat and tidy with artistic touches—everything was in its place, everything had its place. If perchance books lay scattered on the dining table, it would cause a stir in the family. If a servant took off her *chappals* in the hall, she would be reprimanded. If an unfortunate visitor were to balance his umbrella handle against the polished case of the music system, it would be discreetly removed. If toothpaste caps were not capped on after use, there was shame and scandal in the family. Tea sets, dinner sets, crockery, cutlery, were all in perfect order, to be taken out for the right people on the right occasion. My mother was a much-travelled woman, not quite Europeanized, but certainly sophisticated. She was to the manner born, as it were.

My mother-in-law (she passed away recently after the writing of this piece) is a study in contrast. Diffident, gentle, eager to please, the kind to be filled with awe and certainly not to inspire it. She would inspire instead, love and affection. She had started wearing *khadi* from the age of ten onwards and it did not matter to her in the least whether her *sari* was draped properly or otherwise. She does not wear any ornaments on principle, never attends weddings or visits restaurants. Her hair would invariably be worn in an untidy plait, her food habits are exceedingly simple. She would be perfectly at ease with books, newspapers, tea cups, scattered all around her room. I now look back in amusement at how 30 years ago my 'proper' upbringing caused me to be scandalized when tea was offered to the sweeper from the same cup as that used by the family. I remember telling this 'shocking' piece of news to my mother. But I must say that that lady of the Manor House had the grace to laugh it off saying, 'you know sweepers are quite clean people....' Unlike my mother's, my mother-in-law's 'travelling' was confined to her exodus from Karachi to Bombay at the time of Partition.

And yet these two ladies—one a true blue Epicurean, the other a devout Gandhian—hit it off together and became, after an initial period of unease, the closest of friends. My mother-in-law would be very eager to please my mother in every way she could and Mum in turn would feel happy at the care and attention showered upon her. As the years went by, Mummy would spend the summer vacation with us. *Amma* would share her bedroom with her and over their morning cup of tea they would listen to *bhajans* together. In the evening, when *Amma* would return from her office—*The Hindustan*—she would get her *jalebis*, *kajus* and *bhelpuri* (none of which she ate herself due to her Spartan ways), which my mother relished. Occasionally, my mother would admonish her for getting bullied so easily. 'Kala, you must stand up for your rights,' she would advise her.

What they shared in common were of course the grandchildren, but also a certain mutual affection, concern and loyalty. Besides, though they would not have thought so, their progressive views made them feminists in their own right, as my son was to recognize in his writing, many years later.

The two respected each other's differences. I can still picture both these old ladies, sitting side-by-side in my mother-in-law's room, shelling peas and chopping onions for me. Mum could chop onions very fine— like a *bhelwala*, I used to tell her. Today when I chop onions (not so fine), the tears I shed are not onion-tears alone.

In the early years of my mother's visits, she used to be the protector— my mother-in-law, the protected. But by the time of my mother's last visit, their roles had reversed radically. Mummy needed care, nurturing and assurance, all of which *Amma* gave her in abundance. Now, it was Mummy who would misplace things, forget where her belongings were, and while I, forgive me, showed much impatience, *Amma* would set things right for her. Whenever my mother came visiting, even in times past, she would carry with her, a black bag. Every morning she would lug it from my mother-in-law's room to mine, every night she would take it back to hers. 'Mary's little lamb', *Amma* began to call it. Mummy found that very funny and began to call it so herself. But the last time she came to our house, the bag took on for her a badge of identity, an emblem of her own home . I realise now why she had become obsessed with it, why she claimed repeatedly that her home was shedding tears and beckoning her back. That was my mother's final visit to our home. I brought back that bag with me when my mother died, from her home at 'Modern Manor'. My mother-in-law is loath to part from it.

Relationships between mothers-in-law have been traditionally coloured with mutual suspicion, resentment and hostility. At their best, there could be mutual courtesy, cordiality and hospitality. However, without quite idealizing it, I have yet to see a relationship as the one these two mothers, mothers-in-law shared. Perhaps I could modify my own statement. In recent years, I have found I share this same closeness with my daughter's mother-in-law. I know that there might be other reasons for it but I would like to look upon it as a legacy of these two older women whom I love and cherish. More than anything else in the world, it has been her closeness to my mother, that has brought me closer to my mother-in-law.

I would like to remember my mother's death day in this manner. As my mother lay dying, *Amma* sat by her bedside, holding Mummy's inert hand in hers. She would get up, touch the picture of Zarathustra in the room and then touch my mother's face. She did this again and again, and yet again.

My mother died a woman blessed.

Note

1. Nanavati, a handsome, young Naval officer had killed his wife's supposed lover, Ahuja. In the 1960s, it became a celebrated case—a crime of passion. This made Nanavati a hero of sorts.

The Cross a Woman Carries[*]

Urmila Pawar

A woman is a wife only for a while
She is a mother all her life.

Memories of that night sting like a scorpion bite every time I reflect on the nuances of an emotion we call '*sorrow*' ....

It was long after midnight when persistent knocks at the door woke us. When my husband answered the door we realized the visitor was known to us. Standing at the threshold, he whispered urgently to my husband. I wanted to know what was going on—but the messenger's stern face revealed nothing. 'We have to leave for your Mother's at once,' my husband announced. I asked him the reason for our sudden visit. 'She has taken ill, that's all ...' was his only curt reply. 'But that is impossible!,' I argued, 'she was perfectly well when we met earlier this evening.' I waited to know more, but neither said a word. Before I knew, my husband and the stranger were out on the dark road, briskly walking away. In my confused state, I followed them after locking the door in haste.

Mother did not live too far. We were soon at her place. A small crowd had assembled at the doorstep. Sound of piteous wails filled the air and a

[*]Translated by Asha Damle.

nameless terror seized me. I felt as if the ground beneath my feet would give way.

No sooner had I entered Mother's house, I saw her leaning heavily against the wall. She was wailing in wild despair. Around her other women wailed, mourned or tried to comfort Mother. Seeing my baffled look, someone hastened to explain, '*Bai*, we have received sad news—your *Bhai* passed away in Mumbai. Your younger brother has gone to bring his body.'

Was it possible? My robust young brother, so full of life—how could he be dead? Unexpected as the news was, its cruel impact shattered me. I held Mother closer, gazing at her in dry-eyed disbelief. The truth, it seems, had not penetrated my dull brain.

As I held on to Mother, I thought more of her than the brother who had died. Vivid images of our childhood passed before my eyes. It is true, I knew my brother, knew his likes and dislikes. I remembered how seriously he studied, the day of his first job—more than anything, his great concern for our family. And it seemed terribly odd that I should think more of Mother than him. Images of her life flashed past in a strange sequence of events. I remembered the way she appeared after Father's death. I had no memory of Mother prior to Father's death. I was too young perhaps at the time. I remembered our Mother only as a widow.

We belong to the extremely poor Dalit community, from a tiny village known as Phansavale in Ratnagiri district of Maharashtra. In the caste hierarchy, our particular community has a low position and being a woman, Mother was considered lowest of the low. After Father's death our income abruptly ceased, forcing Mother to work for the family's survival. Being a poor illiterate Dalit woman, what skills did she know other than the use of her two working hands?

At the time of Father's death, our family was reasonably well settled in Ratnagiri town. In the first place, our migration from Phansavale was entirely due to Father's concern for our education. He built us a small mud hut in the town's outskirts and began teaching in a local primary school. One older brother had, meanwhile, died in the prime of his life. That was a great blow to our parents. After Father's death, when relatives had suggested that Mother should return to the village—promising her everything, even shelter, it was an act of courage on her part to resist them. We continued to stay in Ratnagiri. Mother worked harder than before to educate us.

Just when we considered ourselves secure, the two deaths, first, my elder brother's and then my father's, dealt a severe blow to the family. As if the branches of a mature, sprawling tree were being hacked down, one by one, for no apparent reason—leaving only the bare trunk. I could com-prehend Mother's anguish ... inconsolable, she repeatedly called out Brother's name. Like a fish out of water, Mother gasped for breath. I shared her unbearable sorrow of losing a son for the second time.

I remember once asking Mother her views on the role a woman plays in the family. As steam rushes out of a kettle on boil, so did her words, 'It is a hard life for women,' she asserted, 'motherhood is a cross the woman carries. It is like committing *Sati* by jumping into the husband's funeral pyre.'

That fiery image had made my mind reel. It was at conflict with the glorified images of motherhood. A woman throwing herself on the burning pyre of her husband—was a mother's lot similar to *Sati*?

Young Hindu widows would be doped and pushed into the husband's pyre in a state of unconscious stupor. As flames leapt to scorch their bodies, women tried to escape. They were forced back by armed men. Mother had compared hapless young *Satis*—trying in vain to escape the pyre—with the pain women suffer in motherhood! Her words painted a chilling picture!

But, watching Mother that night, her words came alive ... she resembled a *Sati* about to step on the funeral pyre. Her head drooped from extreme exhaustion and her throat seemed dry. But grief had numbed all sense of thirst or hunger in her.

The women gathered to comfort her were doing exactly the opposite. With relentless zeal they narrated incidents from *Bhai's* life, rekindling embers of misery. After each narration, the women would resume their wailing or sob and then dab their eyes with *sari*-ends. Sitting next to Mother was a female relative. Her piercing howls were an assault on my ears. How I would hate to cry like her—even though it was my brother who had died. The woman made a crude spectacle of her sorrow, perhaps in her misplaced belief that tearful howls guaranteed peace for the departed soul! Whatever the reasons, the woman's shrill wails unfortunately stirred Mother's grief. Visibly exhausted, Mother forced herself to cry louder. Oh! The excruciating strain of it. And yet, custom expected a mother to grieve publicly and prove her love for the deceased son. No one seemed to remember that one's grief was a private matter.

Those gathered to offer comfort, or console, added to Mother's misery with gory references to the tragedy. They openly hinted that a mother's life was worthless after the young son's death. These people controlled her emotions. That was the way of atonement, a sign of sacrifice worthy of a mother, they believed. Briefly, I had come under the spell of the same value system—we were reminded of the age-old belief:

A woman is a wife for only a while
She is a mother all her life.

That statement conclusively argued that a woman had no existence except as a mother. And it was her womanly duty to endlessly sacrifice for her children.

Amongst the crowd of mourners sat a young woman. She added an entirely new dimension to the meaning of motherhood. 'The young man was the bread winner,' she had said solemnly, 'he would have been a support to his mother in her old age.' I think the woman was trying to appear pragmatic with her statement—saying that the old should give way to the young. Encouraged, another smart man had expressed his opinion: 'Its fortunate surely,' he declared, 'that the father had died before him. He was spared the awful shock of losing a son.'

I had thought to myself, isn't that a clever rejoinder on women's ability to cope with misery all their life! In fact, he had projected a distinctly patriarchal portrait of men, who valued only their sons, believing, sons carry forward their family name and continue the legacy.

Time slowly ticked away that night. Night soon gave way to dawn. A number of mourners had moved out to perform morning ablutions. But Mother lay flat on the floor, her swollen face pale, body crumpled. She resembled the mangled remains of sugarcane squeezed out of juice. Like the rest of us, she would need to relieve her bowels, wash, comb. My suggestion that Mother should get up as a new day had dawned was brushed aside as preposterous. Anyway, I was raring to get up and grab a hot cup of tea. My body felt painfully stiff after squatting on the floor all night. If I needed support, poor Mother, how much worse her condition must be.

The kitchen hearth, I remember, stood cold with no sign of any tea. Women were washing up the previous night's pots and pans after chucking away leftover food. When I returned to the front room, a new group of mourners had arrived. They kneeled next to Mother.

After what seemed an eternity, neighbours came with bowls of rice *kanji*. I took a bowl for mother. It was snatched out of my hands by an aunt from the next village exclaiming, 'What are you up to girl? Your mother cannot drink even a drop of water till the dead body arrives and she pours the last drops of water into his mouth! You can drink what you want.'

Mother lay still on the floor, supported by the wall. At one point, I imagined she looked at me through her puffy eyes. Taking the cue, I passed her the bowl, saying, 'Here, Mother, you need this.' She bit her lower lip and her red nostrils quivered nervously like tender *Pipal* leaves.

Utterly despondent, I left the room heading back to the kitchen. Two cousin sisters were busy gossiping by the stove. They seemed indifferent about Mother's condition. Hearing me say that Mother ought to eat something—not a morsel had passed her lips from the evening before—the irate cousins had exploded, 'A wretched woman indeed to witness her son's death! Why did she not die? But live to see this sad day?' I shouted at them, 'Why should Mother die? On the contrary, she must be nourished at once!,' I had protested in vain. They had accused me of being stupid and naïve, 'You are too young and inexperienced! What do you know about being a mother?'

Once again, loud sounds of wailing startled us from the main gate. A sign that my older sister had arrived. Rushing in tearfully, she reached out straight for Mother. Mother was struggling to sit up. The two embraced tightly and their cries echoed through the melancholy room. As my sister wailed, Mother seemed to say something in vain. Dazed and frustrated, she banged her head on the wall. My efforts to calm the two failed miserably. They continued to cry till they were both exhausted.

No sooner had her tears dried, my sister had quickly removed Mother's ear studs. When I confronted her, she ignored me. Were the studs hurting Mother? Did she asked them to be removed? Or did my sister take them for safe keeping ? Without her ear studs, Mother looked even more stark and lifeless.

More visitors poured in. And as the afternoon advanced, all eyes turned expectantly to the gate through which my brother's body was to arrive. Men talked as they waited, discussing minute details of my brother's death. A familiar refrain dominated every conversation: 'It was better for the old mother to die than live to see her son's death.' A funny looking stranger hovered around every few minutes. He repeated the same thing, in different words: 'I did not visit your family until now. It is unfortunate that my first visit is under these sad circumstances.' And I could not help wonder, if that's the case, why visit us at this inauspicious time? The stranger's words had stoked our smoldering grief. He kept the consuming flames of sorrow from dying as everybody had hoped they would.

At midday, a second round of rice *kanji* was served on plates. I glanced at my sister who shouted at me, 'Don't you look at me to help! My legs are asleep.' Waiving aside my annoyance, I took a plate of *kanji* to Mother, made her sit up and eat the gruel. Turning to my sister I urged, 'Come on, at least help me feed her. She has to be strong.' My sister retorted, 'You are mad to think she will eat, as if she has any appetite!' Her sentiments had been repeated by another voice, 'Your mother seems almost dead. What can you expect when a young son dies!'

Since the night before all those present had unfailingly hammered the same message. And there I was, trying to make Mother comfortable. They were pushing her deeper into the well of misery. When I tried to make her sit, mother shoved me away and banged her head again and again. Tears had streamed down her face, her body shook violently and the breath came in choked spasms. The women had cursed me in one voice. They even chided me with indirect hints, 'Has she no respect for our age-old traditions? How dare she feed a grieving mother?' My sister had shoved me into the cold kitchen where I pleaded with her, 'What traditions are you talking about? Let her drink a few drops of water? How can we sustain her otherwise?' My sister explained, 'If we give her water, she will want to go to the toilet!,' 'We will take her to the toilet!' I had answered at once. She had looked coldly at me before going out to serve food to droves of famished men.

I then came out of the kitchen. Women were filling plates of rice gruel to feed their husbands. My husband came to ask if I had eaten and I unexpectedly burst out crying. Soon I went back to the other room where women were sitting down to gossip. A second sister had arrived with her infant child. She abandoned the child at the doorstep and rushed inside. The drama was repeated in its exact sequence. I picked up the poor, baffled child, about to weep, comforting him in my arms.

Exhausted beyond endurance now, Mother simply hit the floor like a wounded bird. She began to sob anew with the arrival of the other sister. The atmosphere in the room throbbed with fresh bouts of sobbing. People began to recall the last time my sister had come, to deliver her son—who was already a year old. *Son*—the inevitable emphasis was always on *sons*. Someone was mentioning how a certain woman was blessed to have all six sons living, sons who maintained their mother in comfort. These gossip-mongers had discovered one central theme—women with sons and sons who supported aging mothers.

Suddenly there was a great hullabaloo outside. Curious, everyone craned out to find out the cause. The local postman, it seems, had just delivered a telegram. A man of solemn countenance from amongst the waiting crowd came into the room to read its contents. He read, 'The body will not be brought home. The last rites will be performed in Mumbai.'

After reading the wire, the man could not contain himself. Both my sisters rushed to Mother who had passed out after the last blow. But she had quickly regained her self-control to sit upright. Her eyes were dry, the mouth gaped and her voice had turned terribly hoarse. All present lamented the fact that Mother must be the most unfortunate woman— unable to see her son's face before the last rites were performed. They cried in chorus, lamenting the accursed mother's fate on not being able to see her son's body one last time. Hysteria mounted to a crescendo bemoaning the fate of such an unfortunate woman who ought to have died before suffering such a cruel misfortune.

Another woman recounted our mother's awful fate, saying, of her three sons, death had snatched two, leaving only three surviving daughters. We three sisters wondered as to which one of us should have succumbed to death? Each one would have gladly accepted our brother's fate.

As if by miracle, Mother had regained her full strength. She could no longer stay silent. Embracing us sisters, she announced with pride, yet, in a grieving voice hoarse with hours of crying, 'All children are equal in a mother's eyes.'

Those present were shaken beyond belief. All at once the hissing chorus of human voices, the insidious gossip and hysterical sobs were stilled. An eerie silence prevailed. No one could understand that the reassurance Mother gave her three daughters was, in fact, a valiant statement of protest. Silently everyone rose to his or her feet. We sisters helped mother take her ritual bath that has to follow every cremation ceremony.

Two decades later, unknown to me, I was to experience these very scenes in their searing intensity when I lost my young son. As they helped me take the ritual bath after my son's death, memories of images buried deep, floated sharply to the surface. The cross I carried, the pledge at the altar, the image of a flaming *Sati* and the true meaning of Mother's words. I had turned to look at both my daughters, reaffirming Mother's ideals, that children are equal in the mother's eyes.

My Mother's Gardens

Tutun Mukherjee

When I began this paper in December 2004, my mother was alive. My tone was ebullient and I cheerfully shared with my mother what I was going to write. Suddenly, my mother became critically ill and within six months, she was gone. My paper was left unfinished.

A dear, understanding friend, the editor of this volume, urged me to complete the paper for *Janani*—so I started writing again from the beginning, remembering my mother and acknowledging my *matri rin*.

My mother represented the kind of lifestyle and hospitality that was a part of the joint, extended family culture, and which is fast disappearing from our society. The daughter of the owner of many collieries, she grew up in a large household consisting of numerous relatives and dependents. They lived in a small mining town in the dusty and baked Dhanbad–Jharia belt in the erstwhile state of Bihar where the rich deposit of the 'black diamond', as it is called, in the belly of the earth creates an iridescence in the hovering air above it. The dark nights are lit up by eerie fires in the horizon over heaps of coal. The children were housebound but did not resent it because the 'house' extended over several acres of land and they had little acquaintance with the world outside it. It was a self-contained and insulated universe, uncontaminated by intrusive electrical gadgets like the radio and the television. Tutors came home for lessons but my mother and her sisters invariably ran away from the English classes. They knew Bangla well and my mother, especially, was an avid reader of Bangla literature. The parents were indulgent and did not think that their daughters needed to be particular about book-learned education anyway. Later in her life, after I was born to her, my mother was determined that I should get the best education available in town and acquire proficiency in English. She went on to put me in a convent school run by American nuns. My mother was very strict with me and would not let me miss school.

Her marriage to a lawyer transferred her to the rich and balmy land on the banks of the Ganga and into a family of lawyers, judges, doctors and bureaucrats. This, too, was a large joint family that never distinguished between siblings and cousins. But the family was a complex one and the brides had to learn to tread carefully to avoid stepping on others' corns. There was a code of behaviour in place for all to observe, which adhered to a strict hierarchy of age and kinship. My mother learnt to adjust to the transition—from a carefree life to a caring one.

Moving from one patriarchal set-up to another, the girl child became a bride and a dutiful wife and gradually, a mother of three children— learning all the while the lessons of patience, compromise and sacrifice. She tried to inculcate in me the essence of those lessons too, which I never learnt. As a young adult, I did not think that the limited boundary of a nuclear family and a profession, which would eventually be mine would either require or promote the virtue of self-effacement. I regarded my mother's attitude to human affairs as a leftover of the old world charm, not viable in our age of cutting-edge expertise. I was impatient with her, I importuned and urged her to be more demanding and aggressive when dealing with people. But, I guess we were of two different temperaments. She would not change her ways. After her death, all the letters and telephone calls that I received from friends and relatives highlighted those very virtues that I had sought to suppress in her and mourned in her passing, the end of a saga of empathy and generosity.

Recollecting those hectic, stressful, eventful and fun-filled years of her life surrounded by numerous relatives, friends, helpers and servants, my mother often wondered how quickly they had passed, almost in the twinkling of an eye. The later years of her life after the death of our father, when she lived with one of us at our respective workplaces so that she would not be left 'alone' at home, were actually lonelier for her because she was far away from the environment she knew well and was comfortable in. For a woman like her, the pivot of whose existence was her home—the mundane chores of everyday life were totally engrossing and fulfilling. She never desired any other kind of life. It is not an easy task for such people to relinquish the reigns of the household. Yet, my mother prepared to do just that and stepped back to the periphery of the circle of activities when age and widowhood overtook her. When I urged her to write the story of her life to keep her memories vivid, she admitted that it would make a fascinating narrative resembling the fiction written by her favourite novelists, Tarashankar Bandopadhyay[1] and Ashapurna Debi. She claimed that intrinsic to the experiences of her life were the play of emotions and sentimentality, elements of passions and intentions, strains of tragedy and sorrow that might seem to strangers too fantastic to be true. She remembered people who seemed driven by strange, sometimes even obsessive motivations; and others who were generous to a fault. It was as though she were watching many characters enacting their assigned roles in the drama called life. Her experiences combined with the interactions she had with different sorts of people had enhanced her life in some way or the other, she said, and had taught her to accept what life had apportioned for her. But one lesson she never learned well was to be worldly-wise with money.

My mother considered money matters prosaic and dull. She did not want them to spoil the texture of her life. Her imagination and creativity took flight in other directions. When I consider my mother's creativity, I am reminded of Alice Walker's classic essay *In Search of Our Mothers' Gardens* (1984). The title of this paper is inspired by Walker's emphasis on the matrilineal legacy of creativity that is passed on. Walker uses Virginia Woolf's phrase 'contrary instincts' in her essay to describe the creative spirit that her foremothers kept alive and the ways in which they expressed their creativity in a society that gave them few opportunities to do so. Walker explains that her mother had a difficult life, but she managed to keep her creative spirit alive and planted incredible gardens with a variety of blossoming plants. She adorned their simple house with flowers from her garden and brought brightness and fragrance into their lives. For Walker, her mother's garden was magic that made both friends and strangers stop to admire or ask to stand and walk amongst her mother's art. Her mother's garden represented an undying love of beauty and creation, symbolizing the weaving of her creative spirit with nature's hand.

My mother planted her gardens with satin threads, cotton yarn and wool. She spent her afternoons bent over intricate needlework; wove fine cloths of lace; knitted sweaters and stitched quilts. She loved to handle colour: see, feel and match the rainbow hues and weave them into patterns. Her work was impeccable—beautiful and neat, with fanciful designs. She never sat idle. There was always 'a work in progress', something to be kept in readiness as a gift for some one at the many family functions and ceremonies that she attended. She preferred to gift something made by her own hands, with tender care and diligence; and so the act of giving became a sharing of the self.

While I was in school, *Ma* tried to teach me needlework and applied different strategies to extract work from me. If I finished an assignment on time, she would agree sometimes to let me go for a movie; or reward me with a picnic on the river steamer that she would organize with Father so that we could watch the fishermen at work and the river dolphins at play; and sometimes she would let me spend an idyllic weekend with my grandparents at the lovely farmhouse in the village, 30 miles away that was surrounded by woods and had a brook flowing behind it.

I understand now the difference between the colours in the gifts that my mother gave and the colours of the paper with which I can wrap my shop-bought gifts. The loss is irreparable. Despite her efforts, I did not learn to nurture the garden that my mother had tried to plant for me.

A unique feature accompanying my mother's memories was the smell of spices. She was a fantastic cook and could spend hours discussing recipes, styles of cooking, spices and herbs. The way she cut the vegetables and the fruits, the way she prepared the ingredients for cooking were all special. My brother even boasted that he could tell whether *Ma* had cooked a particular dish, by just looking at the way the vegetables were cut. She loved to experiment and tried out a number of variations with different spices. She loved to make varieties of sweets. Father often joked that she would not even wish for heaven if she had unlimited sugar, flour, cooking oil or *ghee* and was left to experiment to her heart's content with *jaiphal, elaichi* and *zafran*. My mother also made jams and jellies, pickles, conserves and *chutneys* of different kinds and those who knew of her expertise would come asking for these delicacies. She supplied us with the year's stock of jams and *chutneys*. I remember that after the rains, an intriguing line of glass jars with their mouths tied with clean white cloth would be placed in the sun. Though we were strictly prohibited from dipping into them, the aroma made us perambulate in the close vicinity of the jars, begging for a taste.

For my mother, the kitchen was a microcosm, a place of power in a patriarchal household, where the woman's control remained uncontested. The kitchen garden was the extension of that space where she grew herbs, leafy vegetables, limes and lemons for everyday use as well as berries of different kinds like *amla*, *amra*, *kudrum* and *kul* that could be transformed into mouth-watering relishes of various types. We loved to accompany her into the small garden. The younger of my two brothers appointed himself as the sentry of the garden to claim the small perch on the guava tree as his *machaan*.

Summer months were full of strong scents. Mingling with the overpowering sweet smell of ripe jackfruit was the fragrance of lychees and mangoes that our parents loved. The state of Bihar has an enviable and mouth-watering variety of mangoes that Father would buy on his way home from court—*jardalu*, *gulab khush*, *mithua*, *langda*, *maldai*, *bombai*, *alphonso* in green, yellow, orange and rosy hues—that would be distributed among all the members of our extended family. There would be mango parties when different preparations with ripe mangoes would be served to tempt the palate—juices, soufflés, *sondesh*, ice-cream, sometimes mixed with nuts and flavoured with different essences of rosewater, vanilla, or *chhuara*. Mother would never tire of learning about newer ways of presenting the old fruit.

My mother went out of the way to make friends with people to learn new recipes. Curiously though, she did not need to write any of them down as I did, for instance, in my sudden spurts of interest. She laughed when I commented on it and said that everything was written down in the little notebook in her mind.

Her reminiscences began very often with the recollection of a particular item she had cooked or tasted on a specific occasion. Along with the different varieties of ingredients used for cooking would move the description of the event, the behaviour of the people and the aftermath. The rich smell of spices permeated her memories and made them palpable. We wondered at the minute details she could recall about certain flavours of the spices used in a recipe and the variations in taste that the change in their combination could bring at different times. The newspaper items that never failed to interest her were the recipes from different places for different festivals and her favourite programmes on television were the cookery shows.

We were pretty sure that Mother's fascination for cooking also served as an excuse for her desire to feed people. In this, she enjoyed the unfailing support of our father. I have rarely seen such a couple who loved to serve food to people. Just as there were *bhoj*s organized for friends and relatives at the slightest pretext, festivals provided the occasions for serving *dahi-chuda* at *Paus Sankranti*; *khichdi-chokha* at *Saraswathi Puja*; *malpua and chholey* at *Holi*; varieties of sweets at *Bijoya Dashami*, for all who came by. In fact, Father always said that one should spare no trouble for one's guests because the latter had not come to be served only *dal-bhath*, which they could very well eat at home, and that to be able to feed another was the greatest blessing of God. They were especially keen on feeding the poor and when Father was alive, on a Sunday every month, a simple meal would be served to the poor and the needy, who came in good numbers.

My mother planted her gardens with love and cared for them through out her life. Even with failing eyesight, when delicate embroidery became difficult, she sat with skeins of multicoloured wool to weave her patterns of joy that she could share with others. Her interest in cooking too remained unaffected by age. Notwithstanding the arthritic knees that would not allow her to stand for long at the stove, she insisted on monitoring the mixing of the spices in meticulous proportions for a particular recipe, even when forced to depend on others to complete the rest of the cooking.

My mother lived a busy and a full-life, but she never considered what she did as significant. She distinguished between her work and ours, always insisting that she worked merely to pass time whereas our jobs were *important*. And that is what we generally tend to think about our work too. We take ourselves and our professions very seriously. I am no different. I regard my work, my job as *important* that (I sigh regretfully) leaves me no time to do needlework or prepare pickles.

According to Naomi Lowinsky (1992) who introduced the concept of the 'Motherline',[2] to fully grasp one's potential self a woman must journey through the biological, historical/cultural and unconscious feminine legacy that gets passed on from mother to daughter to granddaughter and to great-granddaughter. Thus, by reconnecting through the legacy of the Motherline, a woman can discover the full potential of her creativity. When Alice Walker went in search of her mother's garden, it became for her a journey about uncovering her own true self. Her mother was her strength and her role model. Walker discovered while searching for her heritage, that the hidden reserves of creativity were hidden within herself.

I do not know whether the discovery of my mother's gardens will help me locate the lode of creativity within me or not, but the journey has certainly brought me to a crossroad of life so that I may choose to re-organize my priorities if I wished to. It has made me appreciate in a fuller and deeper way the values of life that are truly *important*. It has also made me conscious of a tremendous responsibility—to ensure that the legacy of the Motherline that I have inherited passes on to my daughter.

Notes

1. Tarashankar Bandopadhyay (1898–1971), a prolific writer of short stories and novels in Bengali. He received the Jnanpith award in 1967 for his novel, *Ganadevata*.
2. Lowinsky, N.R. 1992. *Motherline: Every Woman's Journey to Find her Female Roots.* N.Y.: J.P. Tarcher.

Stepmother at Seventeen

❧❧

Maithili Rao

We are all our mothers' daughters. Some of us go on to become mothers of daughters. In that passage, fraught with unexpressed hopes and unfulfilled ambitions, lies my own journey to motherhood. From instinctive teenage rebellion against what 'mother' stood for, to a gradual understanding of that taken-for-granted figure as an individual, comes my own maturity as a person.

There is no precise, magical moment when I saw my mother as a woman … and a unique one at that. A brave, vulnerable girl of seventeen who made it her life's mission to be a good mother to her three stepchildren. The oldest was just 7 years younger than her—in a family that was a paradoxical mix (may be typical of the turbulent 1940s) of South Indian Brahmin orthodoxy and progressive ideas. My journey into fully appreciating the gallant battles, small triumphs, stoically-borne tragedies and final betrayal of her dedication by my father can perhaps never be totally objective because of the emotional baggage I carry as her first biological child. I can only unravel my progression from befuddled amazement at her generation's ideas, to sympathy for conditioned entrapment in stereotype from the 'superior' vantage of my own intellectual emancipation, to deep empathy for a woman who had the courage of her contradictions. Her contradictions were both endearingly funny and exasperating.

She was inspired by Gandhian ideals but couldn't bring herself into letting a non-Brahmin servant enter her kitchen. Our live-in Muslim servant wept inconsolably when she died as if he lost his own mother though he never crossed the threshold of her sanctum and left the mortar and pestle in which he ground the dry *masala* by the door. Intellectually, she accepted that keeping a menstruating woman in seclusion has no scientific basis but she would enforce this humiliating practice in her home, wherever we lived—be it in Hyderabad, where we grew up among similar families or in posh South Delhi, *bhadralok* Kolkata or *apro* Ahmedabad.

There comes a moment that becomes unbearably poignant when you somehow become your mother's mother. It came to me when I turned 48. It hit me that I was precisely the age at which my mother died. Memories washed over me, leaving me limp with emotion ... sneaking up at odd unexpected times like snatches of half-remembered songs ... so many conversations, such heated arguments, the flush of my angry resentment bottled up for long with typical adolescent vengeance, her gentle chiding followed by tearful recriminations, her embarrassing pride at my 'accomplishments', the gut-deep connection I sensed between her and my daughter who was hardly three at the time of mother's death ... how I couldn't stop crying as her sweet, mellow voice singing a Tyagaraja *kirtana* pierced me to my core despite the scratchy sound of a primitive tape recorder ....

I wondered ... almost all memories were from the time I was around eight or nine. Where was the subconscious remembrance of physical closeness, of being cuddled and kissed? Why were they missing, however hard I dredged by mind back over the years? I poured over yellowing albums, permanently curled at the edges. There are a couple of my baby pictures, all by myself but not one being held by my mother. Did we always relate to each other as an older child and adult woman? Why did she always take for granted my understanding for whatever she did? Was that her way of loving me without being demonstrative? I can also never forget that she was demented with grief when the baby of our family, Kitti—who lived up to the charm of being named Krishna—died when he was not even two. I must have been a confused 6-year-old. Intuitively, I seem to have walked gingerly around mother who was hardly aware of anything around her. I also remember the Gita *Pravachan* at home, from which she drew strength and clawed her way back to normalcy. Her melodious recital of the Gita is an intrinsic part of my memory of her. Did she love me with the same intensity as Kitti? I still don't know. What I do know is that a mother's love for her children can't be uniform in expression. Can love be dependency? She instinctively grew to depend on me when I was in my teens, trusting that I would understand why she seemed undemonstrative.

It was around the time I was eight that I knew that my mother was stepmother to my adored *Akka* and two older brothers. I never remember questioning why I called her Kakki like my brothers and sister, not *Amma* or Mummy as my friends did.

It was simply the way of our extended family, living in what was the largest house in the area, sandwiched between two lanes front and back. It was unostentatious but hospitable. *Kakki* was its titular mistress but real power was vested in the hands of *Doddamma* (*Thayiji*) and sometimes the temperamental cook on whom my mother was pathetically dependent. Despite the bustling presence of an extended family that had by now shrunk to just *Doddamma* (my father's widowed *bhabhi*) and her son (he was considered the eldest in the family, topping my oldest half-brother by eight months) living with us, I could tuck myself away with a book in some corner. Maybe I was an uncurious, rather unworldly child, teased for always being buried in a book.

Everyone—relatives, neighbours, family friends—all referred to my mother as Sita or your Kakki when speaking to me. In hindsight, this signals the first battle won by my mother. There was no nosey relative trying to insinuate into my young mind the fact that my beloved *Akka*, who was always there for me when Kakki was busy with her social work at the *mahila samaj*, was not my own 'real' sister. The word *savati* seems tipped with more venom than the more neutral 'step'.

How I came by this knowledge—which ought to be pretty shattering going by all tenets of pop psychology—was so utterly casual that I can't believe it even now. It was courtesy the unsolicited kindness of an inquisitive neighbour whose name I can't even recall. What is imprinted on my mind is the curious darting of her bright dark eyes in her plump, fair face. Isn't your *Akka*'s marriage settled yet? She asked. I don't know, was my usual reply to anything other than school or play. 'Why'll your mother bother, she's after all your *Akka*'s stepmother. She is already 18!', 'But *Akka* goes to college', I countered. She sneered, 'College-geelege! Convenient excuse for a stepmother. You are a kid, you won't understand.'

It sometimes takes a casual encounter to wake a dreamy child to the subterranean tensions coiled under everyday routine. I saw that *Akka* was withdrawn and often, there were teary scenes between her and Kakki.

Akka refrained from redoing Kakki's *sari*-pleats—with the normal admonition of it being inelegantly high—and Kakki's eyes had a pleading look that did not hide the hurt. Much later, I learnt from a gossipy second cousin that *Akka* wanted to marry Kakki's relative—a dashing lecturer—and was hurt that Kakki couldn't persuade him into accepting the proposal. Meanwhile, my kindly *Attha* went around with as much grimness as her good-nature allowed because my parents hadn't accepted with alacrity the readymade match with her son. In South India, it is often customary to marry the *Bua*'s son, if age and other things matched. It so happened that finally *Akka* did marry my cousin a few years later, when they were both in the final year of their degree course.

I now realize that Kakki saw herself more as an educator than a close confidanté of her children—me included. She insisted that I do a few sums, write one essay each in English and Telugu every day during the long summer vacation. Her way of approaching her stepchildren, as a college-educated young woman who got married after her Intermediate exam, was to help with homework and extra-coaching in English. (Kakki's unfulfilled ambition was to do English Honours and the vicarious pride she derived when I completed my Masters in English, was touching.) The beauty of extended families is that the actual nurturing and mothering is shared between the mother and aunts, even if they don't live all the time in the same house. Even more importantly, Kakki saw that the link with her stepchildren's *Nani*, aunts and uncles was kept strong with annual visits. She went out of her way to be deferential to this very gentle and cultured family and they, in turn, reciprocated her affection. If Kakki was perhaps over-anxious to keep the relationship alive by every means within reach, this very traditional family living in Bezwada, accepted the new bride who took their daughter's place (she had died heartbreakingly young during childbirth). Others in my father's family might have tried to play mischief, setting up the children against the 'usurper', but never this family that was so sadly bereaved.

I am now convinced that Kakki saw gaining *Akka*'s trust and affection as her greatest challenge. According to family lore, *Akka* (who was the middle child of three) was supposed to have been very stubborn. Kakki had an easier time with her stepsons. My eldest brother was reportedly a handful, pampered by his *Nana* as the first grandchild. Even as a young boy, he had confidence bordering on arrogance. He also seemed to have imbibed a sense of responsibility as the eldest son and had a very protective side, something that continues to this day. He joined the army after his engineering and was a strutting officer when he came home on visits. My mother cherished the *sari* he bought her with his first pay and he always called her Mummy.

As for the other brother Ravin, Kakki felt that he was the one who was most amenable to her influence because he was just three when she was married. She deluded herself that she had moulded his personality. Ravin was shy and withdrawn. He wanted to study medicine but his marks weren't sufficient and Father refused to send him to Manipal with its high donation fee. As a principled educationist, he wouldn't buy a seat and moreover, he simply couldn't afford it. Kakki knew what it meant to Ravin but she was powerless. No one was happier than her when Ravin got his Ph.D and did postdoctoral work. She shared his disappointment and was elated by his late success.

That's why, she was devastated when Ravin married a Norwegian girl he met in the US. At the same time, she was paradoxically happy that Inger was a good Christian. She felt any religion was better than no religion! She had enough of my atheistic arguments about blind faith and gave in with good grace when I refused to do a particular *puja* during *Shravan*. Little clay oblongs with squared corners, decorated with white dots were to be worshipped in pairs to get a good husband. The phallic symbolism of the *puja* escaped my adolescent innocence but I still relish the small victory of not submitting to what I thought was meaningless. I know a few of my relatives branded me brash but Kakki gave in with good grace. That was something lovely about her. She let us make our important decisions and supported it. The only time Kakki lacked resolute will was in her turbulent relationship with my sister.

Kakki wanted to perhaps over-compensate *Akka*, to never let her feel that things would have been different if her own mother were alive. This obsessive need drove Kakki all her life. Even when *Akka* was a mother of two and they (*Akka* and my brother-in-law were happy spendthrifts) ran through their inheritance, Kakki fought with Father to keep sending them money. She overruled Father's argument that as new parents, a couple had to learn to be financially responsible. Would her mother abandon her if she were alive? There was no answer to this emotional blackmail. I wonder if Kakki ever realized that she might be actually harming *Akka*, by tacitly aiding her dependency on Father's grudging generosity. Giving *Akka* all her mother's jewellery was right but abetting financial irresponsibility to reinforce her own sense of duty was perhaps not wise. That is why, there was always an undercurrent of Kakki's constant need for reassurance and *Akka*'s suppressed guilt in the many emotional scenes I recall. To an outsider, it could be a chapter in a soap opera but for those who felt the ripples long after the storm was past, it was exhausting even in its familiar replay. Small incidents could set it off. Catharsis was a recurring experience.

Though I can now analyse the psychological needs that drove them both, it had the curious effect of making me a detached observer even as a teenager. I was resolved not to get too emotional about the small conflicts inevitable to family life. I also realize that Kakki's efforts to make me thrifty (locking away my cheque book when I started working) and adept at household chores, sprang from deep-rooted reasons. She obviously did not want me to repeat *Akka*'s mistakes and was harsher with me.

Kakki was also determined that I should not be a clumsy novice in the kitchen. Her father was a humble postmaster but he was implausibly ambitious for his first-born daughter. He sent her to Maharani's College, where Kakki even played tennis on a few occasions with a princess of the Mysore royal family and had the privilege of a couple of lessons from the violin maestro Chowdiah. My grandfather had given strict instructions that his daughter was not to waste her time in the kitchen and so when she entered this large, intimidating family, she couldn't cope without cooks. 'I don't want you to do something stupid like washing *bhindi*s after cutting them like I did', she warned me again and again. Of course, she did develop into a reasonably good cook when we lived in Delhi, Kolkata and Ahmedabad, but she was in a flap if more than a manageable number of guests turned up. She was finally mistress of her own house when my father changed from professor to consultant and took up assignments all over India. If my home town was my comfort zone, for Kakki it meant absence of censorious eyes watching her every move. She missed many things about the settled ways of Hyderabad, but she also revelled in her new-found freedom. I don't think she ever got over her insecurity, of being constantly judged, but she did reach a plateau of calm in her final days.

It also dawned on me that her relationship with Father was the primary driving force of her life. Somehow I can't help feeling that she never loved any of us the way she did Father. It was more than a romantic streak that made her accompany him to a science congress, leaving me and my younger brother (I must have been four and he, two) under the tender care of my aunt and *Akka*. *Kakki* got a royal dressing down from her father for neglecting her children but she had apparently no qualms.

What never ceased to mystify me is her worshipful devotion to Father. She believed she was Sita to his Ram (Father's name happened to be Rama Rao). When I was in high school, Father went to the US for a Masters in Chemical Engineering because he wanted to move beyond pure chemistry. It was a period of stress for all of us—financial and emotional. Father opted for premature retirement, innocently trusting the speedy process of pension coming on the dotted line and he gave our large house on lease while Kakki, my younger brother and I moved to a small rented house. By this time, Ravin was in a hostel in another town, *Akka* was married and expecting her first baby and my oldest brother was in the army. *Doddamma* was now mistress of her own house now that her son was working and married.

In those two years, my mother who had never gone anywhere except in a car, took two buses to do the rounds of the Accountant General's office to pursue the elusive pension. She saw it as the travails of her *vanvas*. What astounded me was Father's photograph in the *puja mandir*. I remonstrated with her that father was after all a human being even if he was generally considered a good man with no vices and many virtues. But he is my God, she asserted with an emotional fervour that silenced me. Years later, after I was married, she confided how Father stood by her when part of the family jewellery she was given was stolen on her first visit to her parents. Father simply said he had to sell it to pay off the surety amount for a colleague who fled to Pakistan. For Kakki, a vulnerable young bride unsure of her acceptance, this was an act of divine intervention.

What did such peerless devotion get her? She gave up her music after marriage, bearing the barbs against her college-education and artistic disposition. She had the dedication and courage to resume her music and took up the challenge of a new instrument, the *veena*. She coped all alone, braving financial constraints and emotional loneliness for two tough years. I know how humiliatingly frightening it must have been for a sheltered homemaker (a pretty woman in her early 30s) to ignore the leering looks and speculative glances of an all-male government office to get the pension papers moving.

To the family's consternation and the pained shock of *all* her children, Father married again, barely a year after *Kakki* died—to a woman who answered his advertisement, more an indifferent housekeeper than a companion who was his intellectual equal. To me, it was betrayal of not only my mother but a woman I had come to admire for her tremendous commitment and unflinching courage, who triumphed over her own weakness and difficult circumstances.

It was perhaps inevitable that the family ties gradually disintegrated after Kakki's death. We were taught to admire Father and he was a distant figure for most of our childhood. I got close to him when I helped nurse him before he died of cancer. I saw unspoken contrition in his bleak eyes and that helped allay my bitterness. All of us children rallied round him but by then, we had all grown closer to the families we married into. Kakki was the fulcrum, her weekly letters keeping each of us informed of what was happening to the others. She was the channel of not only com-munication but the centre from which radiated the bonds of family love and loyalty.

Kakki always said she was destined to be an Inter-pass all her life ... education that did not culminate in graduation. Her music remained an unattainable quest for perfection. But I think she educated me into giving space to my daughter, to respect her individuality. And the un-heard music of her love still fills my heart.

Ourselves

————

Motherhood and Me

৵৵

Dhiruben Patel

My Mother—regal and resplendent
With all her jewels and a gracious smile
Reigned over the scene.
I stood in a corner
Enjoying it all
Till someone praised the dinner
And complimented my mother
For all her expertise.
　　　　　—Kitchen Poems (Dhiruben Patel 2006)

When I was a little girl, perhaps about 6-year-old, my favourite daydream was to imagine that I was flying around with nine or ten children of my own. As I was ignorant about the practical side of motherhood, being the mother of many children did not pose any difficulty to me, then. All I had to do as their mother, I imagined, was to teach them to fly!

Alas, sooner or later one must grow up ... and childhood fantasies vanish without a trace! However, I have often wondered, if a vestige of this delightful fantasy has not survived secretly ... I still feel that I would love to have several children and would love to teach them to fly. Not for a moment do I think that actually I have none. As a matter of fact, I do have more than my fair share ... children who speak different languages, from different cultures—and who vastly differ in age. If they have warmed my heart, at times they saddened me as well, although unintentionally. Again, I must admit that each one of these children has enriched my life in his/her own special way. For that alone I am truly grateful.

I was a teenager, when I had my first encounter with the new generation. This came in the shape of a 3-month-old baby whose ailing mother was unable to care for him at the time. This encounter brought home the harsh reality of motherhood. It became abundantly clear that babies had to be cleaned, dressed, fed, dried and made comfortable—with the utmost urgency. Flying lessons could go out of the window, worse still, be dropped altogether. It did not take me long to realize that mothering was a round-the-clock job, demanding expertise and experience, none of which, I admit, I possessed. Nonetheless, I took up the challenge, compensating for lack of experience with my vivid imagination. I tried to think and feel like an infant. I made sure—though not always in a conventional manner—that most of the baby's demands were met. This new adventure took up much of my time—for which my only reward was the infant's angelic toothless smiles. At that point of time, I was quite unaware that I was venturing into a vulnerable situation. My own joy or sadness was not of any consequence. The little creature grew so close to my heart that his happiness and his pain mattered more than anything.

The first steps out of one's own self, I believe, usher in the most important transformations in one's life. It opens up vistas of limitless possibilities. At the same time, it renders you more vulnerable, more fragile. It may add new dimensions to life. The step can make one terribly unhappy or deliriously happy. There is one certainty, however, one is no longer secure within the boundaries of one's own narrow existence. Motherhood forces a person out of her cocoon. There is no going back, neither can the mischief be undone! In fact, it grows like a bad habit. Before one can even realize, one finds oneself entangled in many lives. No man will ever understand why a mother drops everything to answer a child's cry. Women, I believe, possess this innate maternal instinct. It is irrelevant whether a woman has biologically conceived children or not. Physical motherhood brings its own metamorphosis, but since I do not possess first-hand experience, I can say little about it.

The only experience I have had and continue to have, is to reinvent myself to suit the role of a mentor that has been thrust on me. Several youngsters have unconsciously accepted me not only as a friend but also as a mentor. To my woe I have learnt that this can indeed be an onerous task!

For instance, I remember the day I steeled myself into eating *karela* fearing that the children dining with me would also reject it citing my example. Until that day, I had never tasted *karela*. I hated it so wholeheartedly that I refused any meal with this particular vegetable. The situation had now dramatically altered. Eating *karela*s was good for health, I convinced the children. Now I eat *karela*s with a smile and not with a grimace. Suffering mortal wounds secretly! Whatever the opinion of psychologists may be, for me this has been a lesson in self-discipline.

There are scores of little anecdotes like this, more or less painful, the only consolation being that they have been entirely voluntary on my part. I am happy if my efforts yield results. It is not always self-torture and Spartan discipline. The exercise is more or less like climbing a hill— arduous at first, but rewarding in the end. Children helped educate me to educate myself. Their novel approach to life never failed to exhilarate me. I have been as much of their mentor as they are mine. On several occasions, I have benefited from their sage advice and their love has nourished my soul.

I remember the gentle admonition of a nephew. In the process of either climbing up or down a tall *chiku* fruit tree, the boy's leg got trapped between two branches. He sent for me through a playmate. In panic, I rushed towards the tree. And almost immediately began scolding the boy for his stupid prank. He listened to me politely. When I paused for breath, the boy remarked: 'I think you should first help me and scold afterwards.' Oh, how ashamed I was! Pulling the branches apart, I wrenched his leg free. The boy had been so right. He had sent me a distress SOS and there I was serving a sermon! But then adults can be stupid sometimes!

Despite such foolish blunders the children have loved and trusted me. If anyone suddenly falls ill at night, I am woken up first and my advice is heeded. It is my hand that they clutch during the feverish hours of night-long vigils. Children share their little joys or sorrows with me or choose me to arbitrate in their silly quarrels. I did not realize how strong our bond was until an incident during one summer vacation, at Matheran hill station.

I had taken my nephew sight-seeing in a rickshaw. During the ride the rickshaw puller casually asked if the boy was my son. 'No, he is my brother's son', I replied without thinking. I did not notice anything was amiss until we returned to the hotel. For almost two hours the boy did not smile or talk. He sulked with a glum expression. We were worried to say the least. On being coaxed my nephew dissolved in a flood of tears. He pointed an accusing finger at me, 'She told the *rickshawalla* I do not belong to her!'

It took me a long time to explain the delicate intricacies of our relationship to the child. Even long after he had calmed down, his hurt was apparent. 'So I do not belong to you any more?', was his bewildered question. 'Of course you belong to me in a very special way', I assured him, wondering if I was speaking the truth! Such experiences in life convinced me that it was nothing but the truth.

Life can be rather cruel at times. If one finds a shoulder to lean on, one leans too heavily without being aware of it. I might have done the same had I not had a splendidly strong and wise mother. My mother—a brave woman—was entirely self-educated. She knew four languages, was a freedom fighter, philanthropist and the director of the 19th War Council in Mumbai. She wrote and published a short story collection and her autobiography in Gujarati. Despite her multifarious activities and her hospitable nature, my mother imparted a deep sense of security in her children. As a child, I never felt lonely or neglected. Curiously, a reversal of our roles occurred as we both matured. As a girl, I had looked up to Mother and was greatly awed by her many achievements. Were it not for her sunny laughter and abundant love, I might have maintained a distance in our relationship. We remained good friends despite Mother's occasional angry outbursts. As I grew older, I was able to overcome my timid nature. A time came when Mother and I were two mature women getting along marvellously well as individuals. We shared confidences, invited opinions and planned things together. Unconsciously, we were reversing roles. As Mother aged, she grew physically fragile. She needed my love and constant attention. Mother would consult me and follow my advice despite her spirited nature. Slowly, I got used to my new role, taking charge of her spontaneously. At that stage, we had become intimately close. During her last days, Mother had almost become my daughter and I tried to be as good to her as she was to me in childhood.

I have come to believe that it is possible for the magical bond of motherhood to be woven between two individuals without a biological relationship. How else can I explain the devotion and trust constantly displayed for the last twenty years by a woman whom I had known as a brilliant young person for only a few months? She regarded me as her mother.

At first it embarrassed me. But her loving care and loyalty wore down my resistance to a great extent and I have accepted her as one of my many daughters. She is also the one child who has given me the least trouble—not that others have intentionally burdened me with their troubles. Then there are my Irish, German and Himalayan daughters! All three have spent very little time with me but their sincere love has made me forget the barriers of nationality and culture and I regard them as my very own.

After our first meeting, Patricia Donelly, an American woman of Irish descent, went so far as to claim she had found a mother in me! Invitations to visit her in the US keep pouring in. She refuses to understand why I cannot go when the intensity of her emotional need is so urgent. On the other hand, I fail to understand why Patricia, the mother of two grown children, should be so lonely and want to cling to a perfect stranger. Does being a poet have something to do with it? I am sure, however, that she does not need a fellow writer. She needs a mother. It is sad indeed that intelligent and beautiful women like Patricia are emotionally starved. Can it be a result of the American lifestyle?

A German girl—Gretel was her name—stayed with me for three days. She became so emotionally attached that she shed a deluge of tears when we had to part. Neither her husband nor I could lift her mood. We were both nonplussed. After being asked over and over again, she finally said, 'Oh, I'll never see you again! How can I bear it?' 'You may see me, Gretel!' I said quietly. She stopped weeping at once and stared at me. I went on, 'We Indians believe in reincarnation. If you really want to meet me, we shall. If not in this life, then in some other life!' 'Oh Mother!' She held me close for a while then turned her face away to enter the car. Perhaps, she will forget her misery after some time, I consoled myself. I sincerely wished she would—but was I justified in ignoring her cry of anguish? Should I not accept her as my daughter?

Another incident comes to mind. Many years ago I was at Gangotri with a group of pilgrims. It was there that I met my Himalayan daughter. She smiled at me with such sweet affection that I was immediately drawn towards her. That night she told me her life's story, concluding that she was to leave for her husband's village in a few days. After that she did something quite unexpected. She held my hand in a solemn manner, and said, 'You will go away in the morning and forget my very existence. But I love you as my mother. I do not want anything else, just promise that you will not forget me. I want you to remember me and bless me.

Will you promise that?' I hesitated a little. The girl's face clouded over. 'I know you will forget me,' she said. 'I will not.' 'Really?' She smiled. Her face was beautiful. 'Mother, remember that you have a daughter here. I will remember you all my life.' 'But why?' 'Because you are Mother.'

So that was that. In the face of the mountain girl's firm affirmation, I had no choice but to give in. I tried to give her some money on the basis of our new-found relationship. She was visibly hurt by my gesture. Firmly refusing the gift, she said, 'No money, just blessings! And remember, you have promised not to forget me.' 'That I have.'

I have kept my promise. I have not forgotten her nor can I ever forget her. But she has forced me to contemplate ....

This aching need for a mother ... what mystery lies behind it ? Is it a primeval urge over which we have no control? Was it by mere chance that these three women clutched the end of my *sari*. It could very well have been someone else in my place. The important thing is their deep longing for a mother figure. Why do human beings need a mother figure throughout their life while in comparison animals forget their mothers the moment they become self-reliant?

I remember another queer incident in my life—one featuring an elderly Sindhi gentleman. I was visiting Sri Ramanashram with a group of friends. We were all introduced to the gentleman. He was polite to my friends but when I was introduced as a 'Professor', he shook his head vigorously, 'How can that be? She is my mother. A mother cannot be a Professor. She is just a mother. Always a mother.'

He meant well but I was hardly 22 at the time and did not relish the idea of being a mother to an unknown elderly man. Moreover, my friends teased me a little. So I avoided him. But this had no effect on him. Whenever he saw me he would come near with folded hands and ask for blessings. I was too embarrassed and kept my distance. Indeed, the gentleman continued to look upon me as his mother.

The atmosphere at the *Ashram* was meditative and this Sindhi devotee was well known and highly respected. During our week-long stay, though I did not bless him as he wished, I was always civil to him.

If that experience was not pleasant, the Pune incident was even more bizarre.

A friend and I had gone for an early morning walk to the Deccan Gymkhana in Pune. We were absorbed in conversation when our attention was drawn to a young woman standing at a bungalow gate. The mother was apparently having a hard time calming her infant daughter.

The child, just a few months old, was yelling her lungs out. My friend made polite inquiries like a good neighbour. As I had nothing to do in their conversation, I made cooing sounds to the baby who immediately stopped crying. The mother was amazed. It appeared that the child had been crying for a long time. The chit-chat between my friend and the mother being over, we proceeded to move. When the baby saw me moving away she started crying afresh, even more lustily. She made her intentions clear by spreading her tiny arms towards me. Naturally, I had to stop and offer to hold the baby. The mother released her with grave misgivings as the baby leapt into my arms and stopped crying. After a while, the mother became unduly impatient. I returned the child. This provoked a fresh outbreak of wailing, resulting in the emergence of her grandmother from the house. We were in a nice fix. My friend being an older and more experienced woman suggested that we go away. But I did not have the heart to be indifferent to the child's piteous wails. Once again I opened my arms and the child literally flew into my arms. Her crying ceased and she gurgled contentedly.

We could not stand near the gate indefinitely. So we were asked inside, with utmost reluctance. I was holding the baby. Every time the mother or the grandmother tried to take her back, she burst into tears. In my arms she was radiantly content.

I ventured to say, 'Let her sleep on my lap. She can be removed to her cot later and we will resume our walk.' I was too absorbed lulling the child to notice what was happening around me. I felt a sudden jerk, as my friend snatched the baby out of my lap and gave it to the mother. Till then I had sensed nothing. 'Let us go,' my friend almost ordered. 'But the child is still crying,' I protested. The child had indeed begun to cry in a most tragic manner on being separated from me. 'Let her cry,' my friend said sternly. As soon as we stepped out she scolded me. 'Do you understand nothing? Why should you cuddle a stranger's child?' 'A child is a child! Didn't you notice, she stopped crying when I picked her up?' 'Oh yes! Didn't you notice the mother and the grandmother's hostile glares?' 'Hostile! But why?' 'Because of fear. They were afraid you had cast a spell over their child.' I stopped walking and laughed heartily. I had never heard anything more absurd in my whole life. 'Are you out of your mind? Me, cast spells ? This is most ridiculous.' 'You don't understand. Mothers are superstitious. They don't like their children being handled or even seen by strange women.' 'I was no stranger to the child!'

'All the more reason for their fear. Even I was surprised at the child's behaviour. How could you remain so cool?' 'Because I loved her and wanted
her to stop crying. I love children. All children. And I think she loved me
too.' 'Very well, but you will have to promise not to play with any child
till you have children of your own.'

'Impossible! You know I am not going to marry or give birth to
children.'

'That is alright, but why should you put yourself in an awkward
position? Mothers do not like childless women handling their babies.
They are afraid of the evil eye.'

'Oh!' I was rendered speechless after that last barb! Not in my wildest
dream could I imagine being suspect. However, after the initial shock we
walked on and I kept laughing as I walked. The stupidity of the whole
thing was simply amazing.

'I was afraid you would feel bad,' consoled my friend. 'Why should I
feel bad? I love children and children love me. Mothers and grandmothers
may like it or lump it. I do not care one way or another!'

The baby's mournful wail floated across the cold morning breeze. With
a shudder I tried to forget the incident. But through these years, I have
not been able to get rid of its lingering memory.

I have heard women argue that children can be a great nuisance and
that attachment to a child shackles women's personality and curtails their
independence. I am not sure if they are right or wrong.

My personal belief is that love for a child heightens one's perception
and understanding to such a level that one acquires a sixth sense and a
third eye. One becomes wiser and a better human being. Not just that,
one starts to understand and love not merely one's own children, but the
entire humankind. And then in our own way we strive to create a better
world where the children we love can live in harmony ... I am certain
there is nothing more I expect from life.

A Mother, Myself

❧❧

Kamala Das

I had not given motherhood a thought until I became a mother at sixteen.

It was because of my failure in mathematics and the subsequent disgrace caused to the family and clan that I was married off at fifteen to a kind relative. During the first months of pregnancy I suffered from a severe form of morning sickness that brought in dehydration. I was eventually sent to my grandmother's house, pale and green with nausea.

Grandmother told me that girls of our family never even thought of going to hospitals to have their babies. Babies were to be delivered in the hallowed precincts of our home, unexposed to male scrutiny. The middle room on the first floor was chosen for me as it was sunny and cross-ventilated. An old maid servant was allotted to me for helping with the elaborate oil-bath that was prescribed for pregnant women. Her name was Unnimaya Amma—and she had helped three generations of women in our family to go through their pregnancies. She wore no blouse, a flat amulet hung around her neck. She rubbed warmed *dhanvantara* oil on my body till the skin absorbed all of it and began to tingle. She pulled out the recalcitrant nipples of my breasts to prepare me for the suckling that would have to be done after the baby was born. She rubbed *neelibhringadi* oil into my scalp and later washed away the excess grease with a shampoo made by her out of the leaves of the hibiscus. Powdered *mung dal* was applied to the body to remove the medicated oil. Such a treatment softened the skin and gave it resilience. The women at home, my grandmother, mother-in-law and neighbours, pampered me during my pregnancy.

My own mother had told me that labour pains were mild and bearable. I believed her. I read some old Malayalam journals which had run, as a serial, an article on easy childbirth. It said, as soon as the pains began the mother-to-be had to take a hot water bath and relax her nerves. After the bath she had to walk up and down till the spasms occurred after every 3 minutes.

The idea was to avoid panic and tension. My pains began in the afternoon. I put the Victorla[1] on and listened to some old *Carnatik* classicals. My husband's cousins who were my closest friends rushed to be near me when the child arrived. Our family doctor, an old gent named Itty Varghese, came visiting wearing a stripped shirt and a bow-tie and settled down to wait for the delivery. All were in a cheerful mood.

I had no sense then of the agony that I was to undergo to expel the child from within. My friends and cousins all in their teens sat outside my room in the balcony eating sweets and drinking tea.

Till the very last spasm the music was on. Midwife Annamma then shouted out to the doctor that the head was visible. My first son was born in a shroud at 5 P.M. and I had no time, nor chance to scream. My son seemed like a lovely plaything, a living doll for me to dress and feed. Although too young to be a complete mother, I nursed the child and enjoyed the sensation of it.

I have had three sons. While bringing them up I did not even require a God to worship. They filled my life with sweetness. I wrote only when they were fast asleep at night, in the blissful hours when I felt that I had done my duty as wife and as mother.

Children grow into adults. And adults grow out of their need for parents' love. This is a natural and a desirable process. Mothers begin to feel unloved, unwanted. This too is as natural as the graying of the hair and the wrinkling of the skin.

To this day I think of my sons as my young ones and when I meet them at airports, or at my doorstep, I yearn to put an arm around them and kiss them but I control such urges and observe the decorum expected of a matriarch.

Now that they are responsible people on-the-move and impressive achievers, I hesitate to talk of my loneliness when they are around. I feel that I have outlived my use and that I must die to remain for them a sweet memory.

Note

1. A musical player.

A Delicate Bondage

Pratibha Ranade

What the daughter does,
the mother did.
—Jewish Proverb

Fifteen minutes after the birth of my first child, *Aai* brought her to me. The baby was already bathed, powdered and wrapped in the soft folds of her old 9-yard *sari* and looked angelic! Amazed, I touched her. Before I realized my feelings towards her, I slipped into a deep slumber.

Aai made me drink milk, *kanji* when I was in a daze. I really woke up after several hours of sleep when she helped me sit-up, with a special meal in her hand. I could now see the little pink bundle in the cradle at the foot of my bed. I had almost finished my meal when the bundle stirred with a plaintive wail. *Aai* fondly said, 'the little one is hungry.' Before I knew what was happening, my blouse was drenched with milk. I was stunned, and extremely embarrassed. Nine months before the baby's arrival, I was dreaming about motherhood. The reality shocked me.

Why did my body react this way? Only last year, a 19-year-old me was studying for her graduation. What happened to that 'me'? With these thoughts, my eyes filled with tears, tears of shame, self-pity and also annoyance. *Aai* was holding my infant daughter for me. Gentle was her reproach!

And how kindly she coaxed me to accept these new changes in my body. *Aai* understood me too well and made it seem natural. Since then, I have depended on her wisdom and judgement.

'Did this happen to you, when I was born? Did you feel the same way?' I asked her. *Aai* replied with a pleasant smile: 'I was hardly sixteen when you were born. Not a thinking person at all. I accepted whatever happened. Now I am excited, with the arrival of my first grandchild.'

She put the little baby on my lap, teaching me how to feed her. We three, *Aai*, my newborn and I were a close-knit family of emotionally-bonded souls, struggling desperately to adjust to the changed world around us. I was happy to be with both. To me, the image looked like a frame from Ingmar Bergman's film! Or like a Ravi Varma painting. The scene was repeated years later, when my daughter gave birth to her first born, another daughter.

A time came when I had to leave the secure comfort of my parental home and go to my own, hundreds of miles away from *Aai*. Two sons followed my daughter. By that time I had overcome the physical discomforts of motherhood. It was routine work. *Baba*—my husband—being away on tour, I had to look after the kids alone. Feeding, bathing, washing, sleepless nights, endless demands were rewarded with my children's bright smiles, their soft touch, faith in me sparkled in their bright eyes. Everyday brought new surprises, along with frustrations, anger and of course, enormous fatigue. I had to be the nurse, cook, scavenger, playmate, teacher ... there were endless roles to perform. The thought that one day my children were going to become healthy, intelligent, handsome adults, made that effort worth it. I realized that motherhood was a relationship not only with growing children, but with their father, other relatives, even one's neighbours. It meant the food you cook, the clothes you choose for them or yourself. It was a whole new pattern of life.

Sometimes, I wondered—how long does one need a mother? I soon realized, the need for a mother is lifelong. But it is affirmed in different shades, at different times of one's life. One's infancy is totally dependent on the mother. Even when the child learns to walk, it wants the mother to be within reach—to whom it can run to, in times of trouble. This emotional dependency continues till the end of one's life. One may travel the earth in search of greener pastures, but the longing for a mother or, a mother—like a person waiting at home, seems to be a universal human quest. It is strange how every individual craves for independence, but does not want the mother to be free. In the absence of a real mother, due to death or severed relations, one looks for a mother figure in others. For this reason men expect their wives to be like a mother. Men look for protection, support, absolute love, forgiveness and unconditional acceptance from their wives—the very qualities a mother possesses.

All the saints in the *Bhakti* movement in Maharashtra, identify their favourite God as a 'Mother'. The motif is expressed in their poetry. God Vithoba is referred to as '*Vithumauli*' (Mother Vithu), or '*Vithoba-Mazi Aai*' (Vithoba, my mother). In the UN building sprawled over vast acres of land in Geneva, every alternate corner of the building is adorned with a cute statue of a mother and child. I wonder is this symbolic? That the UN, like a mother, takes care of its member nations? Some of the best paintings in the world are on the mother and child theme. However, Michaelangelo's world famous sculpture, *Pieta* surpasses all other portrayals of motherhood. In his *Pieta*, Michaelangelo immortalized the pristine qualities of a mother. She is portrayed as an image of absolute love, acceptance, unconditional forgiveness and a colossus of strength.

Is any real mother capable of possessing these multiple qualities? Is she allowed to be like that? Is it right to make these unjust demands on her? A mother is never just a mother at a given time. Different people have different claims on her. Growing children, for instance, want their mother to be a typical mother. She has to look like and behave like a mother, she must be homely, a bit plump, forever attentive, but *not* meddle with them. Maya Angelou, the renowned black activist, feminist and poet, narrated an interesting experience in her autobiography. Once she accompanied her teenaged son and his friends to a beach. Everybody goes for a swim. Angelou overhears her son's friend commenting on how sexy she looks! She noticed that her son was disturbed. After this incident Angelou decided to wear loose, shapeless clothes that would hide her sex appeal. At the time she was 30-year-old and in the prime of her youth. Her son's discomfort was a matter of concern to Maya Angelou. The experience was significant warning for a young mother.

While the children want their mother to look homely, their father wants his wife to be a super-mom, a perfect hostess and fulfil his desire for an at-tractive, smart, modern life partner. This may be that period in the woman's life when she wants to explore her potentialities. She realizes age is catching up. She wants her own space.

My mother had created a niche for herself, when we were growing up. Although, she was not formally educated, this was never a handicap for her. She read a lot, kept herself well-informed, in fact, abreast of the literary, social and political events of the times. She discussed or argued with father. Sometimes she argued with father's friends, on all contemporary issues. I remember those lively discussions in our home about many sensitive issues of the period. When the need came, she learned tailoring and silently added to the family income without making a fuss.

My father was an activist in political, literary and social movements all his life. As a result, we had a tough life. We had to face continuous social constraints, tensions and scarcity. But *Aai* encouraged us to face it stoically and be proud of Father. He was a strict disciplinarian, a loving father and husband, and socially an extremely respected person. Even then, *Aai* had moments of great despair or frustrations. From my childhood, she would confide in me about her innermost thoughts. Perhaps she did not want to expose herself to her elder sister, who was more a mother to her. Hence, *Aai* and I developed a strong bond of friendship.

At times she would reprimand me like any mother. And I would get very angry. How could she change from a friend to a typical mother? Confused, I failed to understand her at these times. It was only when my daughter was born that we became real friends. There was not a single aspect of my life, about which I had not confided in her, sought her advice, support and acceptance. She was always ready to hear me, at times admonishing me, if necessary. And she explained many things with great patience to me.

'How much I burden you! I am sorry, *Aai*', I would say.

'But it makes you feel better, does it not? I am made of steel, I can take it.' She would add comfortingly, at the same time.

Afterwards, there occurred a great change in our roles. It came at the fag end of her life, when *Aai* was an invalid, I felt as if she had become my child. I would tightly hold her frail body in my arms. I combed and pleated her hair, helped her bathe. Once she sighed, 'We have changed our roles! Now you have to attend to me.' There was helplessness and pathos in her words. 'Are you not responsible?' I replied in mock anger. 'You taught me how to be a good mother, and how to change roles!' My words pleased her no end. I always thought that I enjoyed a special relationship with *Aai*. The rest of my family and siblings believe the same.

This may sound repugnant, but I was happy—relieved would be more accurate—the day she breathed her last. She was in my arms, in her senses. I began to recite her favourite *Shloka*s from the *Dnyaneshwari*.

Extremely pleased, she tried to follow me and next moment she was gone. I felt it was a fitting farewell I could offer my *Aai*. It was a glorious death. With her death, a beautiful and vital chapter in my life shut forever.

It has remained a mystery to me as to how, we as parents, enlighten our children about the power of money? Or how do we make them realize their duties and responsibilities without making it seem like a burden they have to fulfil? And also, how to inculcate values of right and wrong? One day my 12-year-old daughter asked me accusingly, 'Are you always and absolutely right, *Aai*?'

I was nonplussed. For one thing, I would never have dared ask my mother that question. On the other hand, there was some amount of truth in what she said. I could not claim I was always right—though I may make it sound like it was. I had to explain to her that it is always with reference to context that right or wrong had to be judged. Our conversation gave me the distinct feeling that I had crossed the Rubicon.

And there was our youngest son—confused about our financial situation. Sometimes we fulfilled their demands, at other times we did not. So one day he asked his father in all seriousness, '*Baba*, tell me once and for all. Are we rich or poor?' We had a good laugh at his earnest query. We explained to him, that wealth or poverty too is measured in context. It saddened me that our son was puzzled about the power of money at that tender age.

Once I had an argument with my elder son. He could not have been more than ten. He was very angry for some reason. Scribbling a quick note, he thrust it into my hand and left home in a huff. His note stated, 'Dear *Aai*, I am angry with you. I am leaving home, never to return. Don't look for me.' At the bottom he had added in small letters within a bracket, 'I will be back by seven as usual.' I ran after him, brought my son back, hugged and said how much I loved him, how precious he is to all of us, gave him something nice to eat—to calm him down. After sometime, I asked him about the bracketed sentence. In all sincerity he admitted, 'I was afraid you will be miserable worrying. So I wanted to assure you.'

These little vignettes of sharing and caring for each other, remain cherished memories from my children's childhood.

No doubt, we had our share of tensions. Our differences. To balance motherhood and your own individuality is very similar to walking a tight rope. A little extra tilt this side or that and you lose your balance. I remember when I started to do a part-time job, editing a children's magazine and writing for it. My work became a favourite family joke. Was it because my small monetary contribution made no visible difference to our lifestyle? I did not know, but I could see the family felt neglected. They would act difficult. They were used to my being at home all day, even when they were at school. It was only after I received recognition and literary awards, that they appreciated my work and understood my sense of fulfilment. Accepting me as an individual came slowly as they grew into adults.

It is believed that each new generation tries to distance itself from its previous one. I think, this distancing is specific to one's personal aspirations. On the question of social values, the gap is narrowed down to a slender division. My mother forbade us—my sister and me—to read any 'romantic' literature and 'romantic' films were also a taboo. She believed they would corrupt us morally. This made us terribly unhappy. But when she took us to see *Andaz*, a love triangle between big movie stars like Raj Kapoor, Dilip Kumar and Nargis, we were pleased and surprised, wondering at the same time, as to why she made this exception to the rule? *Aai* explained then that she wanted us to realize, how not knowing your own mind or giving wrong signals brings about tragedy for all concerned. She was, in short, educating us. In the bargain we enjoyed the tragic romance of beautiful people.

History once again, repeated itself. I forbade my 16-year-old daughter from reading *Lady Chatterley's Lover*. I managed to hide it from her. But the intrepid girl looked hard, found it and of course devoured the book. I was blissfully unaware of her literary adventure! In any case, she was a rebellious teenager. The code of conduct I inherited from my mother, I wanted to pass to my daughter, in a modified form. Although I had felt constrained, I never had the guts to challenge them. My daughter openly defied me. And only recently she told me about the novel with a mischievous laugh. 'It is such a stupid novel. I did not understand why you stopped me from reading it! D.H. Lawrence had some weird ideas about man–woman relationship.' She may be right. I asked her in reply, 'Suppose your daughter Mukta tells you someday that she wants to marry a man you disapprove of, what will you do?' 'I will lock her up. I don't want my daughter to marry any Tom, Dick or Harry!' was her instant reply. Her reply confirmed that my mother's goals and objectives had been passed on not only to me, but, in turn, to my daughter.

How to protect our daughters from the wicked world, has been a nagging concern for mothers. It must be argued that mothers have to keep their sons away from wicked ways to protect somebody else's daughters. Mothers have to be aware of this responsibility. Much to their astonishment, I told my sons, at the start of their university education and when they were beginning to date girl, that I would murder them if they deceived any girl. They protested, claiming that even girls can deceive. All the same, I was confident they would never misbehave with girls. I knew, I was harsh to my boys, but I had to. I am intensely distressed about the fate of unwanted mothers in our society.

I can never forget that young mother. She wanted to get rid of her child. We were both room-mates. I had just given birth to my son and was celebrating his birth. And this poor woman had not even hugged her first newborn baby. She was desperate to put the child in an orphanage or an institution. She was unmarried, a victim of a misguided love affair. Disowned by both her parents and the father of the child and only 22-year-old like me. I was shocked, overwhelmed with pity and disgust. But as I matured, I realized that the halo around ideals of motherhood is a myth, an illusion. It is the privileged or the fortunate few who may enjoy some kind of benefits.

For very many reasons, motherhood in itself is not as noble as it is claimed to be. It is the quality of our relationship with children that makes motherhood meaningful and honourable. I have discovered that despite occasional differences of opinion, mutual love, respect and trust, not only with your children but with their respective spouses, the foundations of harmony and fulfilling motherhood are already built.

To reach there, I have taught myself to be a little like a steel wire. Ready to be moulded if required, but never losing original shape. I am a part of my children's life when they need me. That gives me ample time and space for introspection. However, a nagging question disturbs me. Would they understand how much I need them? Do they know how fragile and vulnerable I have been all my life behind that mask of a protective, supportive and disciplinarian mother?

'How did you manage with three kids? We find it difficult enough with one.' The children ask me. 'You will know yourself.' I replied, 'As you mature in age and grow in understanding with your children, you will know.' I say to them with a smile.

Perhaps therein lies the answer to my own unresolved anxiety and nagging questions about motherhood in general.

Motherhood: Not a Joke!

❦

Nabaneeta Dev Sen

*For from that moment, therefore
this free woman became enslaved.*

No, it is not. Not when you are trying to take care of two scared little girls all by yourself in a foreign land and looking for a job as well.

It is not a joke even when you are back home, with a fine job, and sending your daughters to a good school, carting them to swimming lessons, music lessons, dancing classes, doctors' chambers and birthday parties in between your university lectures. A single mother on earth needs to have more arms than the 'Ten-armed Divine Mother'.[1] Nor is it easy to be a daughter to a genius mother who is physically invalid but mentally much smarter than you, and who can take care of both you and your children by providing emotional and intellectual support from her wheelchair. No matter how hard you labour, clearly, it is she who remains the superior figure in the eyes of your daughters despite all your back-breaking hard work! No, motherhood is not an easy matter at all, it is hard to take—be it yourself as a mom, or be it your mom as a mom.

As an only child, I was constantly nagging my mother, all my friends had brothers and sisters, why did I not have any? *Ma* told me she had

13 siblings and it was not much fun. So I had pets for siblings and always wanted to have eight children of my own when I grew up. I have conceived four times, succeeded only twice and have remembered the losses as irretrievable. However, I have ultimately managed to have four children as my playmates. Not bad at all if you achieve even half of your goal. And I have to admit that I have been lucky. Each one has made me proud, each one has given me and continues to give me the care and the warmth that parents complain about not getting from their kids these days. Of course, they have a long and varied list of flaws, naturally. And they also have an equally long list of complaints against me, naturally. That is the children's prerogative. And I reciprocate enthusiastically. We fight a lot, naturally. Nevertheless, we are indispensable to one another, no matter what the children may tell you. Do not believe them. Just ask the telephone companies and you will know the truth.

Here are a few home truths about motherhood and me.

The Story of My Motherhood

Quickening ✍

From that day
The meaning of the word, 'throbbing'
Changed for her all of a sudden.

Just as the tiny bluebell ventures out alone
Cracking the hard ice, just as
A slice of orange glow
Falls on one side of the face
Like a shared memory.

Words are fickle, like wealth

They move from one address to another
Changing their character and loyalty.

The features of the word 'throbbing'
Suddenly hardened. It knocked at her door
With the deed of a long-unpaid debt
Secured under its arm, overdue
From a previous birth.

From that moment, therefore
This free woman became enslaved
For life, bonded forever
To a word: 'throbbing'

(*Spandan*, Cambridge. Translated by the author with Carolyn Wright.)

I turned twenty-five in January in Cambridge that year and suddenly
woke up to the fact that a quarter-of-a-century was already spent on this
planet. 'Its time you took stock of your life,' I told myself. I had published
a book of poems at twenty-one, went to study abroad with a graduate
fellowship and got married soon after. After two masters degrees, I had
just submitted my Ph.D. thesis, but I was not a mother as yet! I complained
to my husband, 'Now the generation gap will be more than a quarter of a
century between me and my daughter.' Yes, whenever I thought of a child,
it was always a daughter. I would have been quite surprised and perhaps
not know what to do with him had my first born been a boy!

Getting pregnant was easy. As soon as I knew I was pregnant I started
organizing myself. I bought a pink plastic baby bath from a sale and
having learnt to knit from my East Pakistani friend Suraiya for this specific purpose, I made a pair of tiny pink bootees along with a bonnet with
pink ribbons and a lacy pink coat. And this was before the amniocentesis
days. I had no idea of which sex my baby would be. Since I was a girl, I
could only think of dressing up a girl.

Though an only child, I belonged to a large extended family and had
seen how boys were spoilt. I was constantly reminded by my aunts that I
was not a boy. Even my generally liberal parents who were free of any
kind of gender bias fell into the trap at times. I could understand how a
little girl's mind works. I was not interested in bringing up a boy. I wanted
a girl.

And now I have three wonderful girls. Two from my husband, and one
produced all by myself. A bit like hens, who do it by parthenogenesis.
The first two came to me when I was a young woman, the third came into
my life when I was past my menopause. Motherhood can be so different
with each child.

My mother was thirty-five when I was born, yet, we were very close. I
am what I am today, mostly because of her. But I sometimes wonder
what my mother's relationship would have been with me, had her first
child survived, a perfectly healthy boy, who died out of the nurses' neglect

in the hospital. She hardly ever talked about him, but I knew she missed him. And I know I would not have meant quite the same to her in his presence.

We had bought and carefully studied a pile of books on pregnancy and childbirth, one was on natural childbirth (everything that I do needs some academic support, that is a weakness I shamefully admit to). I asked my doctor about it and Dr Petrie sent me to Addenbrookes Hospital to take Natural Childbirth Exercises. It was a newly introduced course and very few women went to it. It was the time of the Flower Children, Peace Parades, Dr Spock, Maharishi Mahesh Yogi, all the mid-60s nature stuff. The lessons taught me how to relax in body and mind, and convinced me that pregnancy was a natural phenomenon, after all and not a disease. Childbirth was nothing to be afraid of, all the animals went through it without anaesthesia. I learnt that the fear-pain syndrome could easily be overcome if your mind and muscles were relaxed, remembering that childbirth was not a fearsome but a happy moment in your life. If you were unafraid, eagerly looking forward to the experience of motherhood, you would not feel the pain. Or, rather, it will be easy for you to bear it. I thoroughly enjoyed the Natural Childbirth lessons and decided to go for it.

As a matter of fact, learning to overcome the fear of pain was an extremely useful lesson for me. It has helped me later to overcome severe stress and pain of a completely different nature. It was actually a lesson in courage. A lesson in positive thinking.

As the baby began to move within my body, I was unbelievably excited. It was all real, then? A human being was growing, moving inside *my own body*! My baby! Our baby! I was too excited for words, I was so grateful to the Creator for making this miracle possible.

The day my doctor made me listen to two hearts beating in my body, I had to share the excitement of these mysterious activities inside my womb with my husband. I forced poor Amartya to put his ear to my belly. He listened attentively, was much amused, but showed little surprise. The books said it was time for the baby to move and it was moving. He was relieved and very happy that things were going as they should, but not half as excited as I was. I suppose that is the difference between fatherhood and motherhood. A father can not quite imagine the excitement of carrying a life within your body. It was his child, but not growing in his body, after all.

I was genuinely happy, but at the same time I suddenly felt suffocated and trapped. I felt my freedom as a person was lost forever. Motherhood was upon me, with all its glorious responsibilities. I am now the woman who bears the burden of carrying on the species, the generations behind me and the generations after me, all have their expectations pinned on me. Once a mother, forever a mother. You are duty-bound for all time. You can never be a free woman.

I felt trepidations .... Was I good enough to be a mother? Kind enough? Honest enough? Could I make sacrifices? A mother must be all of these. No. I was not fit for the role of motherhood. I was not mature enough, not serious enough, not patient enough, not wise enough, not knowledge-able enough, not informed enough, not selfless enough, not confident enough. How will I be able to guide another human being in her life? How will I ever answer all her questions? I do not know the answers myself! I am a confused and uncertain individual, how can I make a child feel secure? Luckily, I happened to have the wisest mother under the sun, no one could be like her. Surely not me .... Motherhood was too glorious a role to be played properly by me. I felt insufficiently qualified. But the die was cast.

I knew my girl's body had already turned into a mother's. My taste buds and my olfactory nerves had been telling me the news of the change. My breasts were changing shape, my nipples were changing colour, my belly was growing out of shape. The free woman in me was free no more. The poem, *Spandan* (*throbbing*), came from that feeling of entrapment. That was in May. It was a beautiful summer in Cambridge. I was work-ing in the library, living on fruits and cider. The kind-hearted Scottish doctor had prescribed beer, but alcohol and non-vegetarian food seemed abominable. 'A saint must be coming as our grandchild', wrote my mother from home, air-parcelling me a packet of Indian vegetables.

The Earth Mother

Antara 1 &

Antara rising from primordial waters
As the first sun, forever new, forever old
You made me the universe.
History and pre-history filed through me hand in hand

In gradual evolution.
Antara, because of you
I have earned the right to enter
The tenfold halls of my foremothers

Clutching your baby hands in my fist
I have made the future a debtor to me
Antara, in an instant you have filled all time
By your grace I am coeval with the earth today.

(Translated by the author.)

In October, my first child was born in Calcutta. I had rushed home to give birth, so that she could always write while filling in all her forms 'Born in India'. And in fact when the D-day finally came I truly did not suffer the pain in the excitement of giving birth, I did not scream, I did not howl, it was a wonderful moment, my baby was coming at last! Natural Childbirth worked, I enjoyed the birthing process and when the nurse held up the beautiful baby girl for me to see I felt on top of the world. Literally. As I was learning to nurse my baby at my breast (she looked absolutely perfect, like a wax doll, not with red and wrinkled skin, like some newborns that I had seen), I had a realization. Ah! Here I have a mammal, a tiny little mammal suckling at my breast, who started off as a fish swimming in the amniotic fluid in my womb. Isn't that how the earth grew? Isn't that the story of the evolution of the species? Mother Earth took millions of years to achieve this change from the fish to the mammal, and just look at me! I have taken only nine months to go through the same process, the very same experience! I was an equal of Mother Earth, only smarter. My pride knew no bounds. Pleased with my achievement, I wrote the poem, *Antara 1* in Calcutta.

Antara is my first born. In Sanskrit, *antara* means 'in-between'. It also relates to the Bengali word *antar*, meaning 'within', or, 'heart'.

But before that, on our way to India we had stopped in Greece, and at the Temple of Delphi, a group of Italian tourists felt confused by my shape and wondered whether all Indian women looked like that in a *sari*, or was it because I had a baby inside me. A woman gently touched my belly and asked, '*Piccolo?*' Meaning, 'little one'. I decided that was the Oracle of Delphi and my child was named Piccolo. Piccolo is Antara's nickname.

Goddess a Second Time

An elderly nurse had told me after my first miscarriage that had it been a female foetus she would have survived. They are stronger, they cling better to the wall of the womb. The male foetus is weak, it has to be pampered. It cannot take any strain and falls off under stress. (So the pampering of the male species starts quite early and mother nature herself sees to it.) Thank god, our last born, a lovely girl with golden curls, Nandana, knew how to cling to the wall of the womb and also knew when to leave it! In her case too, I had practiced Natural Childbirth and was not howling as was expected of would-be mothers in our Indian nursing homes. Hence, the Matron, not used to these new-fangled Western practices of quiet fortitude refused to believe that the pain was coming every three minutes as my watch told me and did not call the doctor. But when the head appeared, they realized their mistake. So they held my knees together trying to keep the child from coming out, and causing me infinite pain and anxiety, while they waited for the doctor because the doctor would not get his fees otherwise. The seconds felt like hours. My body was getting lacerated. The baby was fighting to be born. But the nurses were holding on to my knees. The rural woman acting as the nurses' maid suddenly wailed, 'Let it come, it will die if you wait any more' ... and forcibly pushed the nurse's hands away. At once my baby stumbled out of my body, silent and not breathing and fell into the waiting arms of the nurses' maid.

But for that rural woman's instinctive reactions and empathy my Nandana might not have survived. At that moment, poor Amartya was *gheraoed* in a meeting at the Statistical Institute.

I was happy to have a daughter again, as was her father. 'Nandana' means 'one who gives joy'. Amartya had sent me a list of suggested names from abroad and I had sent him my list from Calcutta. Nandana was the only common name on the two lists. So the choice was simple. It's a name for Devi Durga. *Goddess, a Second Time* was written in the nursing home when Nandana was two days old.

Songs of *Viraha*

When my first child was a 10-month-old and had just learnt to stand against the wall, I was awarded a postdoctoral fellowship at the University of California at Berkeley, where Amartya had an Associate Professorship and we had to leave Antara behind. I was very keen on taking her along but my in-laws decided she would be neglected if left to baby-sitters and exercised their parental power to convince their son that it was far better for the child to be left behind with caring grandparents whose total attention would be on her, than to be tagged along with busy parents who would leave her with hired help. In the tug of war between possessive grandparents and a possessive mother, the grandparents won. Away in Berkeley, I intensely missed the early process of growth of my baby, her first steps, her first words, her first sentences. I suffered unspeakably.

Her father was immensely busy with his academic work. He had produced several important papers while at Berkeley, of which some were seminal to his book *Collective Choice* which led to his Nobel Prize. (Incidentally, the book was dedicated to Nabaneeta.)

I tried to be busy too. Invited friends, cooked elaborate dinners, went camping and trekking with mountaineering friends. And produced a few scholarly papers as well, which were later published in academic journals in the USA, and got heavily involved with the group of political-activist students who were staging the sit-ins against the Vietnam War, people like Mario Savio, Jerry Rubin, Bettina Apthekar, Myra Jehlen and others. During the Free Speech Movement I was one of those 100 foreign students who were advised to come out of the Administrative Building to avoid deportation (along with Joan Baez who was singing with us to offer moral support) when 800 American students who had occupied Sproul Hall were arrested by the police.

And yet, I missed my child every minute. Staying away from her was like being exiled. I wept everyday. I was obsessed with the pain of being separated from my baby girl.

I now know I was then in a state of depression because I had seriously contemplated suicide during this time, by romantically jumping off the Golden Gate Bridge, as was customary for all depressed young people in California.

I felt deeply deprived, as, I could not participate in the magical unfurling of my baby's consciousness. I wrote a 10-page letter to my child apologizing and explaining my mental state, to be opened after she was sixteen and a decent suicide note for the police, but finally changed my mind, and destroyed the letters. I wanted to touch my child's face once again, hear her small voice, watch her toddle towards me with outstretched arms, a scene that I loved to imagine every night as I fell asleep .... And

I could not possibly kill my poor mother whose whole life revolved around me. If I killed myself, I would be killing her too. (Besides I still had to produce seven more babies!!) That was the first time in my life I had experienced serious depression, both *caused* and *cured* by the mysteries of motherhood.

Both sets of doting grandparents kept us regularly informed of all the fresh developments in her life, but I felt cheated and was jealous of all those who were lucky to witness the day-to-day changes in my child's life. They had written to me that she was talking now. And how! She was talking incessantly like a little bird, chirping away all day long.

I had stuck a picture postcard on my kitchen wall, of a painting by Paul Klee, called *The Twittering Machine*. Immediately, I made a connection between the two. And a poem was written.

Antara 2: The Twittering Machine ❧

I have a picture postcard
Stuck on my kitchen wall

Spreading out slender wire branches
Across a bright blue sky
And setting four tiny wire birds upon them
Mr Paul Klee has created a funny little machine
With a great big lever attached to it
As if
The moment you turn it on
The tiny wire birds will start twittering
Wielding their thin wire tongues

He has called it
The Twittering Machine.

Whenever I see the picture I think of you
Four little wire birds
Are hidden within your tiny body
And the lever is held in your small fist
Before you could start talking
You have become a chatterbox
Our very own little Twittering Machine
The one we have made
Filling the bright blue sky

(Translated by the author.)

But was the Sky Blue Enough?

But was the sky blue enough? Was it bright enough?

The Vietnam War was on with all its human ugliness. Those were the days of the Cold War, the rich nations were competing over their nuclear weapons, there was social discrimination of every kind, as well as environmental pollution and ecological changes and in some continents babies were dying of hunger—in some others factories were pouring out extra milk into rivers. I was not sure I had done the right thing, bringing an innocent child into this world of hatred and inequality. I felt a strange sense of guilt. Was this world fit for children? This loveless, faithless chaos?

This was the mid-1960s. We were worried about the future of human civilization. The earth was turning into a killing field. India was at war with its neighbours. As a mother I felt I had done an irresponsible act by bringing a child into this dark universe, *just because I wanted to be a mother.* Just because I was dying to hold a baby in my arms, to have a daughter of my own. But shall I be able to offer her a secure and happy existence? Who knows what the future holds for her? Another poem appeared. Very different in mood from *Antara 1.*

Antara 5 &

Someday, even this baby will die.

This baby at my breast, whom
I have brought into this world
After a lot of effort,
At the risk of my life. What if
She asks me now: 'For what reason
have you brought me here,
 in this dazzling chaos?
Which grand festival am I here to celebrate?'

I shall die of shame.
I shall die of fear and shame,
I shall run away into the dark,
I shall run away into a bottomless pit of ignorance

What answer do I have for you, my child?

(Translated by the author with Carolyn Wright.)

These were the very feelings that ate into me when little Nandana was born, several years and one miscarriage later. After the initial excitement was over, looking at the cute golden curls on my gorgeous little baby's head I had the same feeling of guilt and helplessness and anxiety all over again. Did I do the right thing? I had performed a divine act once again. This was the closest that one could get to the Creator ... but could I bear the responsibility of bringing another human being into this imperfect world?

Did I have the power to protect her? The poem, *Goddess, a Second Time*, written the day after my second child was born, partly echoed *Antara 5*. It was another document of confusion and guilt caused by motherhood.

In the Middle of Chaos

My niece in Los Angeles has on her wall an oil painting of a mother of uncertain age, squatting on the floor, nursing a baby in her arm and with the other arm embracing a little girl leaning against her. The little girl is bending over her mother like a very young tree, engulfing her mother and the baby in a strong protective hug. This oil painting was done by me in England—when I was trying to find a way of protecting myself and my two little girls from internal as well as external injuries after their father moved out. And the little kids, while holding on to me, were trying hard to provide me with emotional support, as much as I was trying to provide it to them. Those were difficult times for all three of us, the younger one was perhaps too small to realize the extent of the loss, but the elder one was old enough to get permanently scarred. My protecting arms did not go very far, I am afraid.

Motherhood, for me, was no more an absolute bliss, a state specially to be celebrated, since I now felt that the celebration of life was the reason behind all our activities. It was the reason for our existence on this planet. To celebrate life in the middle of chaos.

But how can I control the chaos? And find a pattern in it? That is precisely what art does. But can motherhood do it too? What could I do to make this planet more livable for my kids?

I was living in England, primarily a mother and a wife ... alone with two small children in London, looking desperately for a job, academic or otherwise, being over qualified and rejected for most of the available jobs, like typists, secretaries, supplementary teachers, or salesgirls. I finally got work as a cab driver with a private mini-cab company in Shepherd's Hill where we lived in a pretty flat owned by a friend, now known as Lord Meghnad Desai. The girls were going to school and however much I tried not to disturb their routine, it was, nevertheless, disturbed. The children were confused by the absence of their father, they were tense. The elder one could not sleep at night. The younger one kept complaining. I took them to the doctor for help. I was working hard towards adjusting to the changed situation, trying to put the children's mind at rest and trying not to upset my mother in Calcutta too much, writing comforting letters to her, preparing her for the news.

This was when the poem *Children* was written. It was written in English, which at that point was the language of my life. For those few months there were moments when motherhood became an unbearable emotional burden upon me. I felt abandonment was at the bottom of all relationships and no matter how deeply you loved them, the children were going to leave you as soon as they grew up. That was the rule of the animal kingdom.

Children ॐ

Whirling like tops inside my brain
Leaping clapping shrieking creaking
Upon the rusty springs of my nerve-ends

Children
Each a solitary palm tree
In a desert island

Sucking up subterranean waters
To bear bunches of bitter bronze fruits

Then and Now

Yes, that was how it seemed then. But the children have grown-up, and the fruits are neither bitter nor bronze, but sweet and golden. Thank god and thanks to my mother, both Antara and Nandana have grown up as balanced individuals, confident and relaxed, with precious creative personalities. They are sensitive, intelligent and sociable. Both possess brilliant and beautiful minds. Antara went to Smith College in USA and was later a Reuter Fellow at Oxford. A well-known journalist, she is a columnist for *The Week* magazine and edits and publishes an internationally-known South Asian literary journal, called *The Little Magazine*. Nandana graduated from Harvard with *Magna Cum Laude* in her second year, and went to the Royal Academy of Dramatic Arts in London and the Lee Strasburg School of Acting. In New York, Nandana is a rising star, acting both on stage and on the screen in India, North America and Europe.

And they ferociously love their mother who has innumerable flaws. Despite my daughters' many complaints against me, they maintain unfaltering loyalty to their mother. So, while their *Ma* was rushing around doing errands all day, their *Dimma* (maternal grandmother) was home for them with her wonderful stories and even better goodies and best of all, her brilliant company. My daughters happened to be quite close to my mother. Both my parents were writers. My mother Radharani was not only a poet and a brilliant thinker, but an avid reader and a great conversationalist and had travelled the world. It was both a pleasure and a rare fortune to be in her company. My kids have learnt a lot from her about life and literature, about relationships and about values that matter most.

Accidentally, all four of my children have turned out to be talented writers, following the tradition of their grandparents. Antara has her fans across the world, Nandana too writes very well when she does and so do Pratik and Srabasti who joined the gang later, have also excelled in their fields as writers. (I do not take credit for this.)

Post-menopausal Motherhood

Magical things have happened to me in my life. To get a child of your own after your menopause is a fairy tale come true. Believe it or not, that is exactly what has happened to me. I have actually got a daughter after my menopause. My third daughter, Srabasti, decided to adopt me as her guardian, when she was in high school and came to me on her own from a suburban town. It was about a decade ago. She was a great admirer of my work and knew most of my poetry by heart. But I had no intention of becoming any one's emotional shelter any more as I already had quite a few depending upon me for emotional support. And that was quite exhausting. But I soon realized that this apparently dare-devil teenager, speeding around in Calcutta streets on a two-wheeler urgently needed help. She was seriously disturbed and needed counselling. Clearly a gifted child, she was addicted to books and cigarettes, was astonishingly well-read for her age, was a skilled artist, wrote poetry and loved classical music, but there was a lot of insecurity, pain and confusion troubling her personality. I was leading an independent life in peace and quiet. For the first time in my life, I was living for myself. The house was empty, my mother was no more, both my daughters were busy with their careers, working in different cities far away from home and I was extremely busy keeping up with my double career—both as a full-time professor and a full-time writer. I had had no time to suffer the 'empty nest' syndrome as yet. I found a counsellor for her and a doctor, and strongly resisted accepting her responsibility as I did not think of myself as Mother Teresa. I was afraid she would suck away my emotional energy. But things came to a point when I realized she did need stronger emotional security and a permanent shelter, and I had to do something about it. So I took her under my wings. Srabasti has since become an integral part of my family. She has turned out to be a great charmer, with a fine sense of humour and human warmth and is very close to her two elder sisters. My friends and relatives (in-laws as well) have fondly accepted her as my third daughter, so has my highly discriminating dog. Today, I cannot believe that there was a time when she was not a part of my family and that I did not give birth to her. Having finished university, she is a bright media consultant in Calcutta, a script writer and a budding poet and painter. She has taken full charge of herself, as well as of my health and household matters. Her young friends fill the house with joy.

However, not only am I the lucky mother of three wonderful daughters, but for the last 15 years, I have had a brilliant son as well, Pratik, a talented journalist, editor and an Academy Award winning translator, who publishes *The Little Magazine*. He made me infinitely proud and happy when he dedicated his first book to his own father and to me. I am grateful to Antara for bringing me such a caring son.

Motherhood and Creativity

I am often asked whether motherhood got in the way of my creative life. Well, not in my case. But motherhood did destroy my own mother's creative life, she became a full-time mother and lived her life through me, giving up on being the great writer that she was. And many years later she blamed me for that, giving me a guilt complex and complaining that she had sacrificed her creative life for my sake. I felt bad for her, but I also felt like saying, 'I wish you hadn't! I did not ask you to do it.'

Hence, the one lesson that I had learnt from my mother was that I should never sacrifice anything that I considered dear to me, for the sake of my children, that would be doing them a great disservice. I did not want them to feel the grudge that I felt, 'I wish my mother had not sacrificed her career for my sake.' I am often asked why I did not marry again. People like to think it was a generous gesture for the sake of my children. Well, I always disappoint them by declaring that the children were not the reason. I had not married simply because I could not find the right man. I have had a lot of fun with my children, I have had a jolly good time, never felt deprived (or unwanted by men), I was no saint. I certainly did not sacrifice a possible wifehood for my existing motherhood. Honestly, I am still not brave enough to go through another broken marriage in one lifetime.

Though motherhood was quite a handful, it was not the mother but the housewife, that had disrupted my literary self. Unfortunately, for the poet in me, I was very happy in my marriage and did not miss my creative life at all! I was too excited and too involved with my new multiple roles as wife, mother, cook, driver, scholar and hostess. I was enjoying this many-coloured, many-layered life thoroughly like a dancing peacock and did not miss my writing. My first collection of poetry had come out a few months before I was married and the second came out 12 years later. As I was neglecting one aspect of my life, I was taking care to build another. Unfortunately, that carefully-created home collapsed one morning and poetry, which I had neglected, gave me the ultimate succour along with my academic work ....

Motherhood was good for me. It gave me strength when the world was falling apart, it kept me rooted to reality, inspired me to write, filled my life with colour and meaning. After my return home, my poems were becoming a bit too sad and making readers curious about my private life. So, I found myself writing happy fairy tales for my children and funny family stories about their activities involving me, my mother and the pets. My readers are all well-acquainted with my children's little antics. The funny stories eased our social life. It told the world that not all broken homes were dark and depressed, some could be full of laughter as well. Even in the absence of a father figure, it was possible for a family of three generations of mothers and daughters, all single, all strong women, a widow, a divorcee and two school girls, to have a good life, and lots of fun.

And today my children help me in different ways to remain creative. They encourage me to write, and to travel, they help me think, they help me translate, they scold me if I am lazy and support me as much as they can in leading a playful, mischievous existence.

Motherhood has come in quite handy, I would say!

Note

1. The 'Ten-armed Divine Mother' is the Goddess Durga who was endowed with 10 arms to hold 10 weapons by the Gods in order to defeat the demon Mahisasura.

Learning to be a Mother

✧⌘✧

Shashi Deshpande

People always talked about a mother's uncanny ability
to read her children, but that was nothing compared
to how children could read their mothers.

—Anne Tyler

We learn about motherhood, about being mothers from our mothers. And what were the nuggets of wisdom I picked up from my mother? Nuggets that I stored in my mind all the years until I became a mother myself?

I learnt that a mother is like God. All loving and all forgiving. She is also as sacred as God, therefore, to hurt her is to commit a sin. I learnt that a mother is constantly sacrificing herself for her children—she wants nothing at all for herself, but everything for her children. I learnt that a mother is one's refuge. She is the one person who will always understand and sympathize. I learnt that childbirth is a painful but joyous process—you go through it without shedding a tear. I learnt that love springs naturally and spontaneously in you the moment you become a mother and that nobility and goodness follow just as naturally. I learnt that a mother can never be unjust or unfair, that she loves her children equally. And what was the reality?

I saw, even as a child, that mothers often tire of their children, that sometimes they are so tired that they say things like 'Oh God, what do you want now?' And, 'Why don't you go out?' Or even, 'Get out of my sight!'

I realized that mothers want you to be what you are not and not to be what you are.

I saw that mothers hold out their love like a carrot—a prize for (what they considered) good behaviour. This love is not unconditional and can, sometimes, bewilderingly, frighteningly—be taken away. I knew that mothers can be, and often are, partial and even play off one child against another. And as for being a storehouse of understanding and sympathy, it is wise never to tell one's mother one's real feelings, one's secrets—these can be used against you and become a family joke.

As I grew older, I came to realize a few more things—that mothers can, and do thwart their children's ambitions, they can stifle their children's desires, that mothers who say they want nothing for themselves, try to get things through their children, a mother's sacrifice can become a rope to tether her children to herself, that it can be used as a weapon in the never-ending mother–child warfare.

When I became a mother myself, I knew that childbirth is not only a hideously painful process, but a cruel and ugly one as well—while I do not remember whether or not I shed any tears, I can remember I howled like an animal in pain. The ignominy can never be forgotten—the stretch marks stay forever to remind you that motherhood is achieved only after a painful physical struggle.

I learnt that nothing comes naturally, not even breast feeding. You have to learn how to do it, you have to work at it. And the worst blow of all was that I realized that I didn't suddenly change and become an entirely different person when I became a mother. Except for the burden of this new tie, I was the same person I had been earlier—nobility and goodness did not suddenly descend on me. What was even worse was that I found out that motherhood is a state of vulnerability—you are now wide open to pain.

And then began the doubts, the agonies—was I an unnatural woman? An unnatural mother? Why couldn't I even breastfeed my child? Why did I so often feel trapped? And though I watched every breath of my baby with such anxiety, though I was flooded with joy at the sight and touch of those tiny limbs, though I absorbed every smile with ecstasy, why did I feel I was being swallowed up? Why did I want to bury my head in my pillow and shut out those cries in the night, the cries that, oh God, seemed to have no cause, emerging only to torment me? Why did I look back with such nostalgia to the days when I had been a girl, 'half-savage, hardy and free'?[1] And there was the rage too, rage at the unceasing demands on me, demands I knew it was impossible for me to meet, demands I knew I didn't have the capacity to meet.

When the children grew older, I kept asking myself—how come I, who had told myself that I would never never descend to quarrelling with my children over trifles, was caught in this maddening tangle, this conflict of wills? 'You must.' 'I will not.' 'Why don't you ...?' 'Why should I?' Petty, degrading and endless.

Much, much later, when I could look back on this period in my life with detachment, I could unravel a few of the tangled threads in this snarl. My mother had lost her mother when she had been only an infant and her idealization of this mother-role was a fantasy that she indulged in. And therefore, the guilt that I heaped on myself was because I could in no way come near this fantasy figure.

But it is not just my mother, it's all of us (including, though I don't like the thought, myself) who carry these fantasy mothers about in our minds. The idea is in the very air we breathe. This mother is a part of our lives, embedded in myths and stories. There's the story of the mother who so loved her son she could deny him nothing. And so the son, instigated by the cruel young woman he loved, asked her for her heart. Which she gladly allowed him to cut out of her body. And when he was rushing to his beloved with his mother's heart in his hand, he fell down and the heart said, 'My son, my son, have you hurt yourself?' Which woman can refuse the halo such a story promises all mothers? What child can turn away from the thought of such totally selfless love?

And now, there are the movies. Our own movies carry this idea to the extreme. Movies portray a mother as just that—a mother pure and simple, absolutely nothing else. (It is interesting how often she is a widow, so that she need not even be a wife.) All attributes are squeezed out of her, so that she is shorn of, if I may put it that way, even humanhood, leaving behind nothing but motherhood. For how can you call someone human who has no desires at all, not even the simplest one of hunger. (Have you seen a movie-mother eating with relish? I am speaking, of course, of good mothers!) All her dreams, her desires, her ambitions, her joys and sorrows centre around her children. There's nothing for herself. And as for sexuality, perish the thought. That is blasphemy!

I have laughed at this white-clad unreal figure, I have mocked her and rejected her. Yet, I have an uneasy feeling that somehow that clichéd stereotype has wriggled her way into my subconscious. For why else do I have this sense of outrage when I see my mother wanting something for herself? Why am I so uncomfortable when she shows herself as a human being? And have not my expectations from my children, however much I may deny this, been linked to this figure, this idea of motherhood? 'They owe me something much more than they owe anyone else in the world, because I am their Mother!' So thinks a creature who lurks within me.

Questions, only questions. I seem to have no answers at all. There seems to be nothing but confusion in my mind when I think of myself as a mother, when I put that next to my expectations of my mother. Confusion and anger. These found a place in my writing. I wrote a story called, *Death of a Child*, in which a woman decides to abort an unwanted foetus. Later, I wrote a novel, *The Dark Holds No Terrors*, which has a mother–daughter conflict at its core. Both are wholly devoid of sentimentality, sometimes they even seem, when I read them now, cruel—but they had to be written in this way. 'Why are the mothers in your novels so unloving, so unwomanly?' The question, asked of me at a seminar, astounded me. I had never thought of it that way. 'Perhaps,' I, in turn, questioned the young student, 'you miss the stereotyped images of loving mothers, the soft pliable cuddling types?' I could have also said, what I didn't think of then. How can they be unloving? Only when there is love is there conflict.

Now that the children have gone away to live their own lives, I sometimes get a glimpse of an answer to some of my questions and confusion. When you become a mother, you do not automatically shed all your personality and become just A Mother. You are still the person you were—an individual who has lived and developed for years before becoming a mother. Motherhood is neither sacred nor holy—it is natural. Since, nature wants you to nurture the very vulnerable young life you have produced, it links you to it in such a way that the child becomes an extension of yourself. The tragedy is to expect that link to stay the same way, even after that need for which nature has instilled it in you is over. Nature's goal is birth and survival. No more.

But we are humans, we are different, set apart from the rest of nature's creations. Exactly! Since, we can think, we can also accept the truth that mothers are human, as well as, mothers. And, therefore, mothers can be selfish, mothers can be cruel, mothers can want freedom from clinging—all this, even while they are loving their children and nurturing them. We must accept the truth that mothers can be unreasonable and possessive, they can be cruel, neglectful and sadistic. Hating their children, battering them. Between this extreme and the other extreme of the ideal mother, stretches a long line on which most of us stand. Nowhere on that line is there a point that marks the point of perfect motherhood. Motherhood is something that cannot be calibrated.

Why didn't someone tell me this earlier? Why didn't I know it's natural and normal to feel trapped, to want freedom, to be resentful and angry when you are deprived of sleep, not allowed a single moment to yourself? Simone de Beauvoir in her book *A Very Easy Death* writes of a moment of truth for her when she asked herself why she was so affected by her mother's illness. It is because, she says, the illness and hospitalization had 'wrenched [her mother] out of the framework, the role, the set of images in which I had imprisoned her'. We all do this. I have done it to my mother and my children do it to me. And, therefore, the conflicts and anger when children see mothers stepping out of their roles, when they seem to go against the image the children have of their mothers. I know that I have often thought, 'How dare she!', of my mother for doing a thing I would have considered perfectly normal in any one else. 'You don't look like a mother,' the daughters of a friend wailed when she cut her hair short. Yes, you should always look, behave and respond like a mother. What do I care about what you really are!

All this rationalization about motherhood has worked fine to this point. It's when I come to myself as a writer and a mother that things get even more complicated. Even before I began writing, motherhood affected my idea of myself as a thinking, intelligent and rational person. Was I drowning that self in this emotional morass, losing it in mindless chores? And then, when my younger son was three, I began writing; a casual desultory kind of writing at first. But, slowly it became increasingly important, it began to absorb me. And the problems began. At frst, I was able to contain this very well, like you do with an early addiction, working only when the children were away at school. Housework and cooking became chores to hurry over so that I could use all the school hours for my writing. But writing (or any creative work, I imagine) can be as demanding as children. It wants your time, a great deal of your time. It can be just as possessive as children, keeping you away from others, making you long for solitude, making you want to 'conserve yourself'. This is a struggle for any woman; for a mother it is hopeless. How do I lock out a child and say 'I'm working'?

'When a man becomes an author, it is merely a change of employment. But no other can take up the quiet regular duties of the daughter, wife or the mother.' So wrote Mrs Gaskell, over a hundred years ago, in her biography of Charlotte Bronte.[2] And, therefore, the 'long roll of childless women writers'.[3] But that's no longer true. For women writers, as I wrote confidently in an article once, it is no longer a question of either/or. Women want both—work and family life. This is even more true in our country where there was scarcely any question of choices. I got married, I had children, I began writing—none of these were conscious choices. I drifted into all of them. And I was determined to do justice to all these things. For this one has to pay the price. Can you sit for hours without raising your head when the doorbell or the telephone rings? When the cooker whistles? It is even worse with a child demanding your time, your attention, your love. And, therefore, all the writing has to be done in the 'wretchedly limited working time', as the artist mother Kathe Kollwitz[4] said, one struggles to get it done. You try never to cut into family time. You never work on holidays, you never work during school vacations. You try to work at night, when you're not too tired to work, that is. All writers have to do this. You just have to make choices, give up everything else. 'I will write my books and raise the children: anything else just fritters me away.' When I read these words of the American novelist Anne Tyler, they seemed to echo my thoughts, my actions. I gave up everything else but these two activities. It was a balancing act, something I always thought I did rather well. Until recently, when my son said to me, 'Did we ever disturb you when you were working? I took care not to bother you, whatever my problems were.'

Was this how it was for them? Guilt struck me once again. But in any case, guilt is never far away; selflessness and creativity are uneasy partners. Creativity demands that you put yourself first. And to put oneself, one's work first—is to fail one's children. Children of all ages expect their mothers to put them first. Children, even if they are proud of her achievements, are never very comfortable with the thought of their mother having a life of her own.

Bernard Shaw spoke of the oddness of the fact that people take up the most difficult of all professions, parenthood, without having any qualifications for it. I agree. I feel now that I was not qualified to be a mother. I was short-tempered, lacked patience, wanted freedom, hated to be clung to. I was never convinced of my rightness, just because I was a mother, never confident of my authority. And I lacked the capacity to fool myself—even when whacking the children, I could never tell myself I was doing if for 'their good'. I knew I was just working out my temper. I have been inefficient, confused, unreasonable, tyrannical, screamed at my children, cried on their shoulders, shared my sorrows with them. I wanted to be a very good mother, a friend to my children, always there when needed. I have not been able to do any of these.

But I have rejected the concept of self-sacrifice or any sacrifice. What I did for my children was what I wanted to do. I could not have lived with myself otherwise.

And I have never tried to possess my children—I have been able to let them go. I have seen the fearful things that happen to a woman who is nothing but a mother. Motherhood becomes a monster that devours both her and her young; or, when the children go away, there is an emptiness which is filled with frustration and despair. I have been saved from this because of my work. My children no longer need me, but my life does not seem empty.

Often, when the thought 'I have not been a good mother' haunts me, I ask myself, surely, motherhood is but one facet of humanness? A very special and important part, maybe, nevertheless one part of a whole. And, therefore, to be a fulfilled human being, to try to relate to one's children (and one's mother) as a human being, should be counted as a positive?

I don't know. This idea of the 'special-ness' of mothers, of motherhood, is something we have been toting for so long, it is difficult to give up. To lay down the burden, to feel lighter, would make us uncomfortable. For what do we put in its place? Perhaps, each time I ask myself, 'Have I been a good mother?' I need to add—to be a mother does not rule out everything else in life. I'm a human being first, a mother next. Will that help? I like to think that it will.

Notes

1. Emily Bronte, *Wuthering Heights*.
2. Elizabeth Gaskell, *The Life of Charlotte Bronte* (1857).
3. Tillie Olsen, *Silences* (1978).
4. Kathe Kollwitz, *The Diaries and Letters of Kathe Kollwitz* (1955).

No Baby, No Cry!

❧❧

Deepa Gahlot

Parenthood remains the greatest single preserve of the amateur.
—Alvin Toffler, 'Future Shock'

An ordinary evening. I am having coffee with two friends—a man and a woman. They have known me long enough to know my vehement views on most gender issues. They are not usually prone to making comments on my lifestyle or personal choices—yet, that evening, they tell me I must consider adopting a child.

Surprised, I ask why?

You don't grow up till you become a parent, they answer together.

Who says growing up is mandatory? I argue back.

We are talking in a time, when people are dragged reluctantly into adulthood, trying to preserve their youth as long as possible; what could be the compulsion of 'growing up' in this age?

Our conversation continues for sometime, and except for insisting that being a mother makes a woman more 'responsible', there is not a single point which could make me ponder and admit, that yes, this sounds like fun; or it is an experience I would like to enjoy.

Even if I ignore the implication that I have to adopt because I cannot, or will not, give birth myself, the idea of surrendering my independent lifestyle for one of lifelong bondage is something that I abhor. What flashes before my eyes is the desperate look in the eyes of some of my female friends when their kids give them more trouble than they can cope with. They have to find reserves of patience or understanding and just the right amount of rage to prevent them from strangling their brats. As they struggle to contain yet another tantrum, their expression says it, 'Where did this monster come from?' What's worse is that you cannot return the squalling little fiend back to the sender.

When their children are small, most urban women's careers take a backseat (unless they have fantastic domestic help or helpful relatives), their lives are consumed by the guilt of trying to be good mothers; they spend sleepless nights with the doubts that their kid is not bright or cute nor friendly enough, because *they*, as mothers, have been somewhere at fault. Even when the child grows into an adult, a mother's pressures never ease. Worse is in store—if the child did not make it big, she or he could always blame the parents. Or the children could make a statement of terrible negation: 'I didn't ask to be born.'

With ill-concealed bitterness, a friend had once accused me, 'You live the life of an adolescent!'

That may well be true but I am willing to bet, that any number of women would readily change places with me. Not being weighed down with the inevitable responsibility that comes with the package deal of motherhood is a deliciously liberating state. I daresay it makes you totally fearless. There is, of course, a downside. One must have the courage to be free—there are caged birds that prefer life in the safe cocoons of confinement and conformity than face the challenges of the wild. Both the options are valid, but one of them is continually under attack.

I do not think I am juvenile, and no one, least of all my close friends can accuse me of being irresponsible or flighty. But more importantly, nobody has been able to put forward an argument strong enough for me to believe that motherhood is the greatest experience for a woman. No half-baked emotional claptrap, I would like to know reasons that appeal to my mind. Even with Epidural, someone else to change nappies and a perfect New Man for a husband (rare type, that), it's a commitment I don't want to take on. If motherhood is such bliss, why aren't more women happier? Why do I hear more bitter rants than smiling testimonials from mothers? The exceptions may be women who don't have to do any hands-on mothering themselves!

Is Motherhood its Own Reward?

Of course, popular culture and the media constantly bombard us with messages that proclaim that a woman is incomplete if she has no child; or that motherhood is not just the joyful culmination of every woman's romantic dreams, but an end in itself. Messages telling men that fatherhood is the best experience of their lives are neither frequent nor all-pervasive. Though in the normal course of things, for a woman to be a mother, a man has to be a father—and none of those rosy family pictures suggest that being a single or unwed mother is such a great idea! If the maternal instinct is genetically coded into the female gene, should not the paternal instinct be equally powerful?

Accepted social norms make it appear that a mother is like this saintly creature who should sacrifice her being, delete every trace of her self to play her assigned role to perfection, with no hope of appreciation or reward. No such demands are made on the man.

Films and TV channels constantly deify women, the *Mother India*-inspired goddesses who have no identity except that of *Ma*. The possibility of women choosing not to have children has not yet occurred to the pur-veyors of popular culture, so the childless woman is either projected as the pitiable *baanjh*, pining for a child, or the Westernized, narcissistic vamp who deprives her clan of an heir because she wants to build a career, or maintain her figure (of all the ridiculous reasons!).

It is true, in the past, a husband and child was the centre of a woman's existence, but then there were no other opportunities open to women. If she did not give birth, how would the stay-at-home woman fill her days?

'*Gehne banwao, gehne tudwao*' the unhappy, childless housewife was harshly rebuked by her husband in the famous Guru Dutt film, *Saheb Bibi Aur Ghulam*. What a life that would be—even unwanted kids would be wel-come than the gloomy emptiness of a lonely mansion! But today, if some-one was to say that wiping a baby's dirty bottom is more fulfilling than a promising career, or that struggling to calm a child's embarrassing public tantrum is a more thrilling experience than, say, exploring the wonders of the world, I will say they are either crazy or brain-dead, or both.

We have long ceased to live in the simple world where hunting-gathering was the lifestyle, or families lived in caves and sat around a community fire. There has been an evolutionary change in the minds and bodies of women (and men), and it is possible that women today are just not hard-wired to breed. But nobody is saying it loud and clear, as the very idea of unencumbered, autonomous women probably scares the hell out of conservative patriarchy.

The only point in favour of procreation is that it ensures the continuation of the species. But in a world battling to contain population or face a bleak future with rapidly diminishing resources, there is not such a premium on reproduction. The sheer eagerness with which the species is busy obliterating large chunks of itself, makes you wonder how sincere is this desire for preservation. Also, we are now on the verge of artificially creating babies, so that may no longer be the chief motivation for women to give birth. (Which means, that if women continue to define themselves just as Mothers, they may one day find themselves obsolete.)

Does any other reason for having children hold today? In urban middle-class households, where motherhood is greatly idealized, there is no real justification to have children. Extra hands are not needed to work on the farm. Children do not necessarily look after their parents in old age. Sons seldom arrive in time to perform the last rites of their dead parents. And how many people have large properties or businesses to bequeath to heirs? By the time the kids are educated and married, the middle-class parent would be lucky if any scraps of their savings are left in the bank! While they have sacrificed their little desires and luxuries to give their children the best of what they could afford, kids take it all for granted. Many couples marry and have children because they have nothing better to do, or are afraid of being left alone in their old age, which, as all evidence to the contrary suggests, is the flimsiest of reasons to start a family.

The Myths of Motherhood

The fuzzy, warm, loving, cookie-baking, lullaby-singing image of Mom keeps coming out of various media, ignoring the fact that several research findings and books (Thurer 1995; Badinter 1981; Douglas and Michaels 2004), have established that the Maternal Instinct is not natural to all women, mothering does not come automatically to women and the perception of motherhood changes according to time, social and economic circumstances. (The very attitude towards children has altered over the centuries—depending largely on prevalent economic conditions.)

There is more debate, nowadays, on men's supposed inability to be monogamous than on the issue of obligatory motherhood. Women are made to feel inadequate, selfish, guilty and a whole gamut of negative things if they rebel against the conventional roles cut out for them.

Women who decide to be childless are far from the stereotypes of work-driven careerists, selfish individualists or 'ultra feminists' who scorn family life, according to research supported by the Joseph Rowntree Foundation (1998). But these stereotypes of childless women continue to thrive and persist, forcing women to fall into step, whether or not they want to. Despite post-women's movement soul-searching, the stranglehold of female conditioning is just too severe to be broken.

Solitary Motherhood is Not Bliss

We do not live in bucolic bliss in large houses in the comfort of a joint family, where women had a support system and kids grew up amidst grandparents, uncles, aunts, cousins and helpful neighbours. The urban nuclear family has made motherhood fraught with stress and loneliness.

Without domestic help, it is impossible for the urban mother to get any respite from the relentless demands of mothering. And despite the pretence to equal parenting, it is always the mother who has to perform the dirty, monotonous work.

Look at the image that pops-up when you say Motherhood—one of a tense, frazzled, scolding woman trying to keep her brood nourished and happy, while they cook up all kinds of new tortures for her. Fatherhood, on the other hand, sounds really cool and jaunty! Fun and games, or picnics and fond indulgences. I am reminded of school, when my pre-feminist mind protested as we girls had to take cooking classes while boys got to play cricket; girls had to learn sewing while boys enjoyed themselves with carpentry and clay. Preparing us for our future as potential homemakers, seemed like punishment, while the guys had fun.

A lot of women, undoubtedly, are genuinely fulfilled by motherhood. Some women have kids in a state of panic (what if the biological clock runs out of batteries?), probably marrying the wrong guy in haste for that purpose then repenting at leisure. But there are many women who have no maternal instincts whatsoever. And it takes great guts to admit that; even more courage to refuse to be cowed down by pressure and have kids. Saying that you don't want to have children, makes people look at you as if you were the wicked witch in person—a self-absorbed, life-effacing, ogre. It is easier, rather, less painful to conform. However, many women who have kids do not necessarily like them, and many women who like kids, may not want any of their own.

The nurturing instinct, a generosity of spirit that makes some people love all humankind and do what they can to make the world a better place, is unisex—not confined to women alone (just as indifference or brutality towards kids is not confined to men). As somebody rightly said, having children makes you no more a parent than having a piano makes you a pianist and the mothering skill is not routinely passed on from mother to daughter through the genes.

Watching my own mother go through the jitters every time I stepped out of the house, her single-minded devotion to my well-being, her sacrifice of her own talents and then trying to live her life through me, her incurable anxiety, caused me immense dismay. It was impossible to live up to her expectations of an ideal daughter. It was not too little mothering that bothered me, but too much. Several women of her generation must have gone through this kind of schizophrenia—poised on the cusp of an era that demanded self-effacement even from educated and talented women, while simultaneously laying out temptations of career and the realization of personal ambition. It was both cruel and unfair. I think, that may have prevented her from forcing me to make choices that did not suit my free-spirited temperament. It could not have been easy for her to give explanations to the immediate circle of people that we call 'society', if they asked her why her daughter was 'abnormal'. Luckily, there was no immediate family around, and my parents had no social circle to speak of, making it relatively uncomplicated. A huge source of support is my progressive father, who is a truly radical individual, ahead of the times. Add to it the mind-your-own-business culture of Mumbai. In the end, after a woman has passed the acknowledged marriageable age, people speculate behind her back, but leave her alone—they can't very well expect her to have illegitimate kids, just to live up to social expectations!

The Biological Bells Don't Toll for Me

I was described by a former boyfriend as a closet mother.

Kids are drawn to me. I am the repository for the angst and secrets of numerous friends, complete strangers in buses and trains confide their problems to me—something I have never been able to explain. I am a ready band-aid for any inner wound and a godmother for all manner of human strays, but I have never had the nesting instinct. I don't go all misty-eyed and gooey at the sight of babies; never coo to infants in prams, and find myself unable to smile benevolently when kids make a spectacle of themselves in public.

After they have passed the age when they pee in my lap, throw up on my sofa, drool on my clothes or want to 'do potty' in the middle of a party, I get along with kids very well. I like their energy, boisterousness, sense of wonder (somewhat diluted by TV) and excited prattle. When they are able to have an intelligible conversation, they are treated like sane human beings—I hate baby talk, cute lisps and have no tolerance of needlessly unruly behaviour.

In fact, you can enjoy children more if they are not your own. Kids like adults who race and wrestle with them, much more than those who pinch their cheeks and say, 'Cho chweet.' I am favourite auntie to many friends' children and that is precisely because I do not have to live with them and spend most of my productive time picking up after them (literally and figuratively!).

By the time kids reach that delightful stage when they talk intelligently, they are also old enough to start judging their parents and continue to do so all their lives. With competitiveness inborn these days, plus media and peer pressure at an unhealthy high, parents are never rich enough, thin enough, smart enough, famous enough to please their kids. Recently, a friend's 5-year-old told her, '*Ma*, get off my back and get a career. All moms go to work.'

By the time children are in their teens, parents are redundant, except as human ATM machines. Like in the good old days, children can no longer be relied upon to be the panacea for all ills for their aging parents. After investing so much in parenting when their best years are spent, what if realization dawns too late, that they were handed a bogus deal? So, if couples step into the minefield of parenthood, they should know what it entails. An informed decision must be made after considering all aspects of the matter, since there is no chance of a change of mind later. But we are almost always presented with a tempting 'chocolate-cake picture' of family life. It's as though there is a conspiracy by families to keep building on the chain of misery, so that the consumer base of the multinationals and large corporates remains intact.

The pressure on women—and I am talking of a social class where women have multiple choices—to have children, starts much too early, before they are mentally ready to decide whether they want to assume the permanent mantle of motherhood. Recent research has shown, that taking today's social and cultural norms into account, the ideal age for woman to give birth is 34. But social coercion does not ease up for that long. What if the woman has an enjoyable and well-paid career by then, which she doesn't want to give up for the hassles of traditional family life? What if the fear of a destitute and lonely old age doesn't worry her?

By the age of 34, I was confident that motherhood was not for me. I am quite happy being the eternal adolescent. No apologies and no regrets.

References

Badinter, Elizabeth. 1981. *The Myth of Motherhood: A Historical View of the Maternal Instinct.* London: Souvenir Press.

Berry, Mary Frances. 1994. *The Politics of Parenthood.* USA: Penguin.

Douglas, Susan and Meredith Michaels. 2004. *The Mommy Myth.* Free Press.

Hrdy, Sarah. 2000. *Mother Nature: Maternal Instincts and How They Shape the Human Species.* Ballantine Books.

McAllister, Fiona (with Lynda Clarke). 1998. *Choosing Childlessness.* UK: Family Policy Studies Centre.

Thurer, Shari L. 1995. *Myths of Motherhood: How Culture Reinvents the Good Mother.* Penguin.

Our Children

More a Friend

❧❧

Jyotsna Kamal

The child, tiny and alone, creates the mother.
—Ann Stevenson

A fortnight back, almost when I was typing this piece, a funny incident took place. Chetana's father, whom I divorced nearly 13 years ago, was visiting us. My ex-husband, by the way, remains a good friend. I was extremely depressed that day. And he seemed a little too sharp with me when I expected compassion. He tried to point out harsh realities, asked me to be introspective and learn to take care of myself.

And there was my daughter, pleading on my behalf like a friend. She appeared completely in control of the situation. Chetana bluntly told her father to stop advising me, and go back to Australia. She was capable of taking care of her mother, she assured him. Even though her engineering examination was round the corner—making her, naturally, tense.

I developed a special relationship with my daughter early in life. When I was 15-and-a-half, I got my menstrual periods. And then it abruptly stopped for six months. The delay made mother take me to the family doctor. I do not remember going to him before, though we were in Bombay for three years already.

As we entered the dispensary, I saw a print of Michaelangelo's painting, *Mother* on the wall. I looked at it and remember being thrilled. I imagined a baby girl hugging me and sucking my milk.

This beautiful relationship with my mother came to a tragic end soon after that incident. Mother, a talented and intelligent woman, passed away suddenly when I was just eighteen. Some strange incidents in the next four years forced me to reconsider my options about marriage and motherhood. I no longer wished to marry; in fact, I had developed a repugnance towards sex. This could be due to my conservative Indian upbringing, otherwise, I grew up in a progressive environment. I did not want to marry but wanted a child—to be precise, wanted a daughter. And relate to her as I did with my mother. I tried hard to fall in love with my professor—many years senior to me and hoped to conceive a girl if I could without sex!

I gave birth to my daughter when I was twenty-six, after a love marriage to an idiosyncratic, but lovable fellow, 3 years older to me. He too nurtured many crazy ideas. For instance, he decided the name of our daughter long before she was born. Chetana if it was a girl and anything else if it was a son.

Come to think of it, I actually have three daughters. The one I birthed, Chetana, now eighteen; besides her, there are Jyoti and Sneha. Jyoti is a comrade friend's daughter. The comrade was a committed activist, a loving father but as a husband, he was a drunkard and a wife-beater.

Jyoti lived with us for two years and little Sneha, the daughter of another family friend, stayed for just a month. These girls were a part of our family. When it was just the two of us, a single parent–daughter unit in a spacious flat on the beautiful plateau of Farmagudi (Goa), I realized from time to time that Chetana and I were more friends but no less mother and daughter.

At the time of delivery, Chetana's father was keen on witnessing the event. After a 10-hour wait he went out to refresh himself. In that 10 minute absence, I delivered. I remember pleading with the nurses to take me to the operation table, which they chose to ignore. So I walked by myself and lay down even as I felt the head of the baby emerging. Dr Banu Koyaji arrived finally, made a small incision resulting in four stitches and Chetana was born within the next few minutes. I noted the time when the doctor bundled her out. It was 8.16 on the night of 30 November 1976. The doctor and nurses thanked me for causing no trouble. The real credit should go to Chetana for an easy childbirth.

She does not give me much trouble even now—on the contrary, I have given her plenty of trouble in the last few years. At her birth, I felt that a real friend was born to me. Yes, from the first signs of pregnancy she was a friend. I enjoyed good health till the day of the delivery.

By the time we decided to have a baby—after two years of marriage—we were active members of the Communist Party. Some friends in a women's group noticed I was expecting. Through my husband they sent me a message to abort the baby saying I would cease to be politically active with a child. I replied, 'You may say what you like—not only will I go ahead with the childbirth but I will also stop working with you.' I was convinced that my becoming a mother would not come in the way of working for the political party. My example inspired other comrades like Anjali Mathur, 'If you go ahead with a child, we will follow you.' And truly they did—Anjali Mathur gave birth to a boy and later, a girl. Meena Menon has a son.

I would like to point out that just as we should have the freedom to marry or remain single; we should enjoy the freedom to have a child or not. And even if one spouse wants to dissolve the marriage, their marriage should be dissolved. But for a child the process is not reversible and both parents have to be responsible for the child, which is rarely the case.

After childbirth, I stayed with my elder sister in Pune. Chetana's father was a full-time communist activist and the party was banned during Emergency.[1] My sister fed me with all sorts of good things and got a bottle of cow's milk daily to help me breastfeed. But my little daughter could not consume all the milk I produced.

After the third day of delivery, I had slight fever and terrible breast pain. I lay with the pillow under the breast and fell asleep. The milk oozed out on the bed. When the nurse came, she scolded me for spoiling the hospital bed linen. And my newborn daughter watched this theatrical scene with a mischievous grin!!

Chetana was a chubby baby right from birth and did not even give me any 'teething' trouble. I breastfed her till she was a year-and-a-half. She was only 20 days old when warrants were issued against her father and me. We had to hide underground. My sister pleaded, to leave the baby with her. But Chetana was a brave girl and chose to be with me!

We hid in a remote village of Pune district for days. It was a very cold month. On the fifth day, I must have caught a chill after a bath, or while washing clothes, and passed it to Chetana. She began to have green motions.

The doctor said that this was a symptom of cold. I argued it could not be true. She asked me who did the washing? I replied it was I, as we had no servant. She advised me to stop immediately. Chetana recovered in no time.

But in a few days she was restless again, crying endlessly. An old lady, our next-door neighbour scolded me for exposing a small baby in cold weather. After her feed, Chetana slept for seven hours that day—a record at her age when she needed to be fed after every three hours. I had no clue how to bathe a baby. And so Chetana had no bath for 10 days! I think, Chetana had a right to protest against this as she did.

It was an ordeal to give Chetana a bath. On the first day, I was terribly clumsy and Chetana registered her annoyance aloud. But soon I grew confident—how radiant and cheerful she looked after a hot head bath everyday.

And when Chetana was three-and-a-half-months-old, she took part in her first *morcha*. By then the Emergency was lifted and both of us were working in the village. Actually, Chetana led the women, who participated for the first time. She was constantly passed from one hand to the next. Now she was with the women who were leading the procession and in another five minutes, seen with someone else at the end of the procession, cheering all. We had *gheraoed* the *tehsil* office 10 kilometres away till evening and won the demand of starting the EGS (Employment Guarantee Scheme). But in this mêlée, Chetana's gold chain, a gift from my mother-in-law, was stolen. I was very upset but Chetana consoled me with her angelic smile.

In yet another *morcha*, she was right in the heart of the demonstrations. The *morcha* reached its destination when the leaders were giving speeches. Women were applauding as two of their demands were granted. Many more celebrated with new *sari*s. There was a loudspeaker and people sang songs on the way as they shouted slogans. Suddenly, the local landlord's *goonda*s descended on the *morcha*. They had planned to kill the three leaders of the united front, Kastakari Sanghatana, the local branch of the Janata party and a Gadga Kranti Sena (on NGO) leader, who was an old enemy of the landlord.

I was breastfeeding Chetana at the rear. By a sheer act of bravado, I rushed to the front and tried to catch a police inspector, who was hitting party members. They were stunned to see me with a baby hanging at the waist. The leaders escaped in the meantime and the police *lathi*-charged and used tear gas on us. Our smart cowboy friends responded by throwing stones from the road. What perfect aim those young kids had! Nineteen goons and few policemen were injured but Chetana and I escaped unhurt.

I remember someone grabbed Chetana from me and went into hiding. The police caught him and gave him a good beating. By then Chetana was sleeping in the arms of some other old fellow. He brought her back to our village safely. I returned to the village 6 kilometres away worried about Chetana's feed. And there she was happily entertaining strangers, after a drink of fresh goat's milk. She upstaged me in making friends and staying cool at critical moments.

When she was two-and-a-half-years-old I sent her to a local *anganwadi*. She required a pencil a day. When I wanted to buy one for her, she said she would buy it on her way. That day I decided to follow her. She had gone hardly a distance of hundred metres when I saw her buy a slate pencil and eat it on her way to the *anganwadi*! I knew it was time to give her calcium tablets. Medicines poured in for her—enough to start a free dispensary for the village kids.

Chetana's idea of entertaining us was to eat the cat's share of dry fish, or chocolates with their wrappers, demand fruits like guavas and bananas, devour six at a time, or chirp non-stop with maids in 9-yard *saris*—all with perfect ease!

Once, when she was about five, her father and I had a heated argument. Chetana intervened by making comic acrobatic gestures—her childish attempt to stop us. She continues to carry the solemn responsibility of mediation between us.

At times, Chetana was liberal and at other times, possessive of her mother. She was only six when we divorced. And she continued to stay with my mother-in-law in Bombay. I decided to be a paying guest in Bombay and complete my postgraduation. I would bring her over on weekends. If friends came to visit me she drove them away. Soon she made three girlfriends near by. I had the added responsibility of entertaining four girls—take them to a park or a children's drama. I never remember buying Chetana gifts or anything. But she was deeply attached to me. Adverse comments about me always upset her.

After our divorce, her father decided to marry the very next year. Chetana broke this happy news to me. She even suggested I should remarry on her birthday as her father was tying the knot three days prior to it. Casually adding, 'It would be so nice to have two mothers and two fathers.'

Whether we are together or not, my daughter and I have been close. When I brought her to Goa and admitted her to the fourth standard, I had to rush for a UPSC interview in Delhi the very next day. I left her with a friend for a week. I was terribly anxious, but not Chetana.

Staying at her grandparents, she was pampered by both. Her grandpa would take care when grandma was away at work. As a result her daily schedule suffered. Chetana's visit was postponed when she went to England with her grandma. In the meantime, I had a brilliant idea. Jyoti was in her tenth standard—I promised her that she could study in Goa if she secured a first class. Jyoti and her mother Sugandhi arrived in Goa by mid-June. Jyoti had settled herself at home when Chetana returned from England. To be honest, I was apprehensive, how Chetana would react to Jyoti's presence. Seeing Jyoti at home she remarked happily, its nice to have a *Didi*. Her remark made Jyoti happy as she had two younger brothers back home.

Both got along well. Chetana picked up good habits from Jyoti, cleaning and tidying, decorating the house or working in the garden. She complained about my shabby ways in exasperation. Seeing her reprimand me, a friend once joked, 'Jyotsna may be a fearless woman but she is afraid of Chetana!'

Life was wonderful for Jyoti, Chetana and me. Goa suited us. The blooming garden around our house made a perfect setting. There was one problem—Chetana was a late riser. By the time she woke up, Jyoti had left for college and I had to tie Chetana's long hair before leaving. I had two lectures daily from 9 A.M. Her late rising disrupted my class schedule. I remember beating Chetana once about it—but Jyoti and Chetana resolved the issue. Jyoti agreed to wake her up before leaving and also help comb her hair. My part of the bargain was to give the girls Sunday head baths.

Jyoti, a hard-working girl possessed a calm temperament. The two girls made friends with the entire campus. Both learnt cycling together. Jyoti generously offered the new dress, her own birthday gift before she wore it, to Chetana. Jyoti left us after her twelfth standard. Her father, our comrade, had just passed away. She felt responsible for her mother and the two younger brothers. In those two years, Jyoti was with us, she gave us more than we gave her. For one thing, she taught us the gift of patience.

Once it was Chetana's turn to help Jyoti. A good sportsperson Jyoti was keen to participate in her college events. She, however, missed the first round of sports trials because she was caught up somewhere else. The teachers refused to take her. She came home crying and it was a sight watching Chetana comforting Jyoti. Both burst out laughing when Chetana fed Jyoti, reversing their previous roles.

Life changed dramatically for Chetana after Jyoti left. I was forced to move into a one-room kitchen quarter at IIT (Indian Institute of Technology) Bombay hostel for my for Ph.D. We would fight daily as that little place cramped us. She did not keep it tidy and we had people coming over who made a mess of the flat. She missed Jyoti greatly. But soon Chetana was her old self making friends all around—the watchmen, hostel cooks, maids, a group of children and even the fellow who ironed clothes! Many of the girls, M.Sc. students came over for one thing or other, be it medicines, gas, fridge requirement or cooking ingredients like curd, salt, wheat—thanks to Chetana. Her birthdays turned into a hostel function with many friends. At times, she worked with our gardeners, learning from them and later, would in turn, advice them! So life went on ....

Chetana took time off to visit her grandparents on weekends. She was in her eighth standard when she participated in a *Dandia Ras* with the IIT hostel girls. And curiously, people asked—from which IIT department did she come? She had matured fast in that environment. Jyoti and Chetana went to Goa for her admission to the eleventh standard and Chetana stayed back with my cousin sister for two months till I joined her. She showed a lot of independence.

In the meantime, I had translated and published the autobiography of Mirium Makeba with a grand release function attended by noted people like Deena Pathak, Vidya Bal and Pandit Jitendra Abhisheki. Chetana was upset at not being able to attend the function. She went through a few newspaper pages, with a hurt expression and remarked, 'You mentioned everyone's name, thanked them but what about me? I helped you to type it out on a computer, I co-operated with you.' I realized sadly that I taken her for granted because she was my daughter.

During one of her birthdays, the only festival celebrated at home, I was too unwell to celebrate. Not waiting for a formal invitation, her friends began to pour in. Finally, she and her father—who religiously attends it—hurried out to get a few things to celebrate. On such rare occasions, she would be angry and would refuse to talk to me.

When her twelfth standard examination was two months away, Sneha came to stay with us. On a sudden impulse I had promised her father to take this 5-year-old under my wings. Chetana was terribly upset as I did not inform her about Sneha's family, mother, father, two younger brothers who were going to come to Goa when I would be away in Bombay. They invaded her peaceful life. Not used to village sanitation both the kids would trouble her and their father, our comrade, laughed at her discomfort. When I returned after eight days, things eased up a bit for Chetana.

When the family left, Sneha stayed back with us. I found Chetana was still irritable. She resented Sneha calling me *Aai*, hugging me and asking for special attention. Chetana was upset when I got her a new birthday dress. She even resented our long after-dinner walks with our dog Caesar or Sneha's fondness for the pet cat. During my absence, Chetana beat or threatened her. The little girl never complained but I noticed her mimic Chetana whenever she was alone. And then Sneha would disturb Chetana during studies. In a month's time, however, Chetana regretted having behaved the way she did. I had reminded her of Jyoti and how sweetly she treated her. Chetana slowly took to Sneha. But, one fine day, Sneha's father came to take her back saying her mother missed her.

Much later, Chetana admitted being wicked with Sneha. She thought that was the reason the child went back. After that my niece Poonam came to stay with us during her eleventh year. The girl had lost her father in an accident. It was Chetana who helped Poonam study and come to terms with her father's death. She was a true *didi* to Poonam.

Today, Chetana is an engineering student in my college and once again our house overflows with her classmates who live in the hostel.

It is worth mentioning, that she compliments me for not losing my head. The truth is, sometimes only in extreme instances, did I raise my hand on her. Last year, she joined karate and pushed me in anger. That was a lesson for me. She has become stronger than me and her martial skills would make me pay heavily if I were to lose my temper or beat her. The only time she can be demanding is during examinations. She even complimented me for being able to teach her better than her father. He is impressive but does not bother to explain, or ridicules her for not knowing simple things. In her own way, Chetana is proud of both her parents.

After her father went away to Australia, she asked me, '*Aai*, who is going to take care of my father in his old age, except me?' In the same breath she added, 'I can stay with you all my life but with him no more than three days at a time. But as he grows old, he will need someone to take care of him. You can take care of yourself I know.'

Thus, she is less of a daughter and more my friend. Chetana is now a Kinetic-riding, smart young friend, but still cries like a baby when I apply tincture iodine on her wounds, like the other day, after a minor scooter accident.

One instant she is a friend and the next, a daughter. But then, I too, behave like a mother and receive a friend's response when I need it, as you have realized from the moment I began this story.

Note

1. The infamous 1975–77 Emergency was authorized by the then Prime Minister of India, Indira Gandhi. Many political activists, journalists had to go underground for harbouring 'anti-government' views.

Letter to My Children

❦

Mallika Sarabhai

What the daughter does, the mother did.
— Jewish proverb

My dearest Revu and Anahita,

Lying in bed for the past few days, feeling terribly low with raging high fever—I have been thinking constantly of you two. And in my imagination, talking to you from the inner recesses of my being.

You are growing up incredibly fast! Yet it seems as though just yesterday, I had told *Amma* in a firm voice, 'I don't want to marry. I don't want children—don't like them.'

Years slipped by. During that period, I met several men, became involved a few times. But I was firm in my determination of having *no children*. All at once, there was a marked change in me—this is after I met Bipin. Soon afterwards, I wanted to have *his* child.

You know how close *Amma* and I have been. In many ways, especially in my ideals of mothering, *Amma* has been my main reference point. But my growing up was not always very smooth.

৯৶৻ঌ

I was always closer to *Amma* than to Papa. Why that was, I am not quite certain. When I was 7 or 8-year-old, I would deeply resent the time *Amma* wasted being with Papa. I did not want to be far from her. Going to school, as a result, became a daily trauma. This was not because I did not like school, but I hated even temporary separation from *Amma*. I, literally, followed her in everything. I wanted to be exactly like *Amma*. By the time I was 12 years old, my individual personality gradually emerged. And with it the umbilical cord was gently loosened. Suddenly, there were things I wanted to do, people I liked—but *Amma* did not. At the time, I could see no reason for her rigid attitude. I understand today, she saw it as disloyalty on my part. Being as wise as *Amma* is, she knew our growing apart was inevitable. I too may have felt disloyal, or resented the situation that caused us to drift without any apparent reason.

As though overnight, new rules were imposed. These rules were explained to me much later. I was *not to* stay out after midnight. I was *not to* go out alone with a man. I could go out *only* in groups. I could, however, meet anyone, for as long as I wished, *only* in the privacy of my room at home.

'Papa and I have chosen to live our lives in our own way. But we have to protect you till that decision is yours. People talk unfairly. Before you know you will be stuck with a reputation beyond your choice, or understanding.'

I knew my parents held distinctly different views from each other. *Amma* was the stricter of the two. She was also the practical one. She coped with day-to-day problems, braved their consequences. Papa could afford to sound more liberal, afford to talk more in terms of ethics or principles. But he did not have to deal with the daily task of monitoring his daughter's evenings-out, picnics and frequent jam sessions. That was a painful phase against visible boundaries—of my being misunderstood and also confused. In the period that followed, I had boyfriends and love affairs.

And after that came the terrible devastation of Papa's unexpected death. We had a horrible feeling of being sucked into quicksand. Papa's death made me realize that I had to fill the empty space. It came as a bolt. But I had to look after *Amma*, hold the family together emotionally.

Over the next few years Kartikeya, *Amma* and I took turns to wear Papa's mantle. We continued to do that in our different ways. By then, *Amma* had become less strict. She seemed even less prudish. She was both Papa and herself in her one-self. Her psychological horizon expanded wide. Never did we hear her say, 'Had Papa been alive, we could have done this.'

I seem to have embarked on an endless voyage of several decades as I drift through these experiences and unspoken conversations. Often I sit to wonder, what are the imprints on my psyche as a child of my extraordinary parents! Or what shall I pass on to you, my children?

ॐ

Regardless of whether you do the right thing or not, I love you and will continue to love you. Whether you become heroes or stars—my love for you will never go away nor change. At the same time, I am aware of my responsibility—which is to groom both of you into becoming 'good' and complete individuals.

Why did I say 'good' like that—with such defined emphasis? What exactly are the implications of being good?

We live in a world of dissent and mindless violence. Things I hold dear have long vanished; things like—tenderness, laughter, compassion, a sense of adventure or sharing, fighting for rights, thirst for knowledge and finally, the aspiration to become a human being who can light lamps and open doors for those less fortunate. As I write this to you, disbelieving faces rise into my vision, contempt rings loud in my ears. But, my sweet ones, nothing else matters in this life, nothing.

We have been very fortunate. It is, of course, true that our wealth gave us a great sense of freedom. But what is more fortunate for us are the values our family stood for. For more than a hundred years, your ancestors, great grandparents, grandparents and we, in our own way, have fought for freedom. We fought to improve people's lives, for human dignity, for self-respect. Our legacy to you then is that invaluable tradition. In addition, you must remember to keep an open mind—a mind that hears and thinks—perceives and rethinks, when required. Retain an openness to admit 'I was wrong', if you were. I cannot protect you from the sorrows of this world or from getting hurt. Even if I could, I would not. From my own life, I learnt that much good is born of pain. Decisions that shaped my life, gave birth to my creations have, without exception, been born of immense pain. The searing pain of childbirth, for example, and after the remission of pain, the sheer joy, when the infant you gave birth is laid at your breast.

As long as I am alive, I shall hold you in my arms, heal your bruises, help reaffirm faith in yourselves, whenever you are in doubt. Just as *Amma* does for all of us, unfailingly.

That is the source of our life-energy. The knowledge of being loved and trusted unconditionally, of having faith in each other. That, my children is a wealth like no other riches in the world.

There have been times, and there are bound to be other times, when you may feel let-down by us. For you and Revanta, Papa and my separation brought anguish that you could not comprehend. I was struggling with terrible anguish myself. My only hope at that time was not to turn against your Papa in the erroneous belief that he was to blame.

In a relationship, it is a relationship that goes wrong. The process fails rather than the individuals involved in that process. I have tried to be open with you about what I understand to be the reason for our break-up. Some of it, at one level made sense to you, then. Some of it, may make sense as you mature.

You are both extremely talented children. But at no point of time does your talent give you the right to behave arrogantly. Many of us have talents and our accomplishments are highly visible. Those who appear dull are not essentially people to be disregarded. Behind apparently ordinary lives are some extraordinary people. Behind the most humdrum existences are the most astonishing stories of love, courage, faith or humanity. My little angels, never judge others, either as individuals or as a group. That, I consider wrong. It is a difficult lesson to keep in mind at all times. We fight against this temptation everyday. Sometimes we succeed, at times we may not be so fortunate. But, never give up.

Once again, I will go away, far from you on an extended trip to perform abroad. I know you hate these periods of separation. You, Revu, don't utter a word. You express it through tense physical manifestations. And you, Poo, will howl, at once begin to count on your little fingers and toes, the day of my return home.

Leaving you both at home is heartbreaking for me as well. But I have to continue my work, as much for you as for myself. One day, you may begin to value my work. When you do that, your hearts will swell with pride. I too cried when *Amma* frequently left home and it was many years later that I became inordinately proud of her work. Remember, your understanding is important to me.

There is another reason. In order to create, in fact, to put my life, my goals, my art, into perspective, I need time to be with myself. I need space.

Everytime I am with you at home, our love and laughter clouds the clarity of my vision. I yearn for solitude and a tiny space of harmony within myself. I find solitude and space in the physical distance these overseas tours offer.

I use the time away from you to reaffirm my art and rekindle my values. Without this opportunity to be centred I would be a lesser mother to both of you. With my love, always,

—Ma

Paint and Nursery Rhymes

Rekha Rodwittiya

I wouldn't have had kids if I thought I had to be perfect for them.
—Lucy Ferriss, American writer

I was twenty and two days old when my son was born. Nothing prepared me for the wonderous moment when I first set eyes on him!

My son Mithun was rather a long baby—bald, except for the ring of hair at the nape of his neck, he had a puckered red face and yet, I thought, he was the most beautiful infant I had set eyes on. I watched him that entire night. Mithun's birth was to play a decisive moment in my determination to chart new directions in my life. I wanted to be a mother and a painter at the same time. And I wanted to be both on my own terms.

Being a single parent for the first seven years of Mithun's life, never posed any problems. I experienced all the terrible difficulties associated with single motherhood, encountered prejudice. But felt no threat nor did they overwhelm me. It was the beginning of my journey in understanding my own identity and relocating it within a wider radical perspective.

In the intervention of change, the attitude of imbibing change is something that is logical. I realized that parenting was not out of a handbook or a manual. Nor was it a mere replication of your life on to another being.

I chose to look at all the things that surrounded my son and slowly added or subtracted along the way.

Even with an open mind, you need to have a structure that compounds what you believe to be important, or else there would be neither yardsticks nor parameters of knowledge. My life experiences gave me the ability very early to know what I did not want to be, allowing me to reconstruct modules and test their viability.

My life has two distinctive components, separate yet, interlinked. The professional and the personal. I separate the two, not to indicate differences of values, but because they manifest different attitudes. My feminist ideological stance requires me to exemplify these values in a particular way. However, these same values will be offered to my son as another way of perceiving life, but with the hope that they would become, by his choice, part of his own life schema. Far too many parents spend their life using their children as mirrors. When ultimately the image does not correspond with the one prescribed or hoped for, you find bruises of disillusionment spill over on both sides. What we then end up offering the child is a legacy of conflicts.

I was puzzled by the different roles I had to play with my parents. I have heard on countless occasions the pride parents take in pro-claiming that their offspring are their best friends. I do not believe children ever want to be thrust into this permutation, which compels another nature of loyalty and confidences. My relationship with Mithun has established our placement with one another as that of mother and son.

Mithun is aware of the pain of both personal and outer confrontation, but he has experienced the gift of its liberation too. In the 16 years of his life, he had to fight many battles along the way ... some of these he shared and the others I sensed. Hurt and pain come with these encounters and though it has been hard for me to actualiy witness these moments, I resisted the temptation to cast an illusion that life can be simplified by offering my love for him. What I have done instead is to create a corpus of knowledge for him that strife and struggle are part of an individual's journey, necessary in honing our potential and a process by which we affirm our inner strength.

I have always been a good juggler of time. There is nothing that I cannot accommodate, if I wish. I have worked long hours, day and night, painting furiously in between household chores, writing, teaching and being with Mithun. These were very stimulating years and Mithun's presence helped me create a focus, a responsibility and a purpose, which is his greatest gift to me.

Leaving him behind with my mother for two years, when I had to leave for London on a scholarship was the most difficult decision to make. He was three-and-a-half and I could only see him again when I returned after the completion of my M.A. I remember breaking down and crying on receiving my degree. A tumultuous surge of emotions raced through me. However, I have a switch in my head that turns off any kind of pain and channels it instead towards a positive learning experience. Regret, I think, is a wasteful emotion that breeds personal insecurity. This has an impact on our children and such an emotional climate generates feelings of guilt in them, leading them tragically to believe that all negative occurrences are their fault. I did not want to place Mithun within such a tragic context.

My self-growth and Mithun's upbringing, run parallel. My own life has to appear purposeful, nay meaningful, to me. I believed that only if I respect who I am, could I, in turn, offer Mithun a holistic vision of life. The meaning of love has to be deciphered personally if it is to manifest itself to another. Emotional stability, discipline and the setting of limits in a relationship provide vital anchorage to impressionable minds. I believe anarchic freedom does not sit well on the shoulders of children. What I have identified as imperative in our lives is honest communication—besides speaking we learn to listen to each other too.

Surendran and I fell in love when Mithun was 7-year-old. Mithun knows he has a biological father. A man he has not met and I did not think it was necessary to impose another person on him just to fill this role. It was left to Mithun to orchestrate the pace of Surendran's entry into our lives and integrate with us. My love for Surendran was founded on mutual respect and I was, as I remain till today, endeared by his tranquil sensitivity that has none of the male aggression and dominance I detest. Mithun found an intimate friend in him that did not threaten his closeness with me.

I have witnessed many women slowly fade away in their tortured need to prove their maternal sincerity. Indian society has been the main culprit in creating an over-stated definition of motherhood, that wrongly equates the renouncement of a woman's personal needs as a sign of proper parenting. I remember feeling personally anguished as a teenager when I encountered mothers who advocated virtues of such an attitude.

A woman must be economically independent. Herein lies the key to her true emancipation and dignity.

I know Mithun has benefited from my deep commitment to painting. He is confident that I have a world other than the one we share together. This leaves him free to search his own passions and forge his own commitments, without me endeavouring to fulfil my life via his choices.

Memories accumulate as children grow. From my own childhood experiences, I realize that memories are not constructed from a single vision or perspective. They differ dramatically from person to person and each single interpretation of that specific memory is truthful. I have always wanted Mithun to have total freedom in recalling his memories in terms of his own interpretations, and not be burdened by appropriating them to be something he believes will please me. Mistakes are part of any human process. To awe our children into the falsehood that we are not susceptible to failing, would make monsters out of virtue.

I used to hold Mithun's hand after he fell asleep as a tiny baby. I was terrified of the dark and in holding his small fist in my palm, I can still recall the protectiveness that would push my own fear away. On my return from England, he used to have a little corner in my studio that was his space. Having my studio at home I would often, after his evening meal was over, play music and paint for an hour. He would occupy himself with his own drawings. It was comical that he imitated my postures and gestures! I would crack up laughing and leave him in serious doubt about my sanity!

I remember, too well, Mithun standing on our small studio balcony one afternoon throwing my foreign colour pencils to a group of young children below, who were needless to say, happily grabbing pencils as they fell. When I calmed down and asked him his reason for doing this, his reply was that he was sharing what we liked ...! Mithun has always made me laugh. This is indescribable joy.

I have encountered many obstacles in the attitudes of people regarding my being divorced and a single parent. The most painful perhaps being the lack of solidarity from many young women in India, especially during my college days. The memory of such indifference has prompted me to lend support to young people, and women in particular, struggling with their lives in any way. Mithun has imbibed this desire to help others. It is uplifting to see him thinking about the consequences of those who are needy and how his intervention can support them.

I am happy to have my life patterned in a certain way and to then create the choices to make new patterns from it.

Mithun's life, his spiritual well-being and all that is associated with him will remain of utmost concern to me. But if I am to really love him, then I must begin to let him go, set him free to make his own patterns from existing ones, as he chooses. Each different stage of a child's life is not unlike another chapter of a book, the complete story only falls together at the very end.

The Colour of Hibiscus

⊰⊱

Nita Ramaiya

Here goes my classic Mum
who knows how to solve every sum.

'I could not sleep at night,' said Aneri.*

'How many horses did you release in your dream?,' I teased.

'How many? Oh! my mind was hopping from one thought to the next,' she said.

Aneri had not slept for the past three nights and I was relieved to find she did not worry about it. She was in fact, overjoyed by her fresh enthusiasm towards a future she had only dreamt of. Aneri sat in the chair next to me and said, 'Let me tell you, I will surely go mad if we do not succeed in this matter.'

This was true. The child we were about to adopt was suffering from jaundice and was unlikely to survive. Aneri fainted and fell like a log of wood on the floor when the social worker of the institute gave us this news.

---

*Aneri is the narrator herself, giving her own account in the third person. The unnamed 'I' is the author's husband who witnessed the process—and the initial stages of adoption and motherhood experienced by 'Aneri'.

She observed great control over her emotions in the tense period preceding the adoption. Actually, when she planned to adopt a child, I asked her to think about it for a few days before taking any decisive step. Hardly after three days or so, she sat near me, and said clearly, 'I gave it a good thought, now it is final. We will adopt a child. Look, we are not going to have a child of our own. Isn't that right?' 'Hmm ...' is all I said, not knowing what to reply. 'And we want to have a child in our life—you agree?' She demanded. 'Hmm ....' 'In that case, let us adopt one; and the child will be our own; yes, our own,' she said. 'Alright but it may not be as simple as you think ... and what about going for Artificial Insemination, as the gynaecologist suggested?,' I blurted out. 'I don't approve of the method as it is not congenial to Indian culture, which emphasizes the sanctity of the marital relationship. Come to the point,' Aneri insisted. 'Look, I have given it a good thought—specially to all sorts of issues related to the adoption of a child,' Aneri continued. 'For example ...,' I asked. 'All sorts of issues: Is it necessary or obligatory, or even compulsory for a woman to be a mother? Is being a mother a woman's fundamental need? How sincere or strong is my own aspiration to be a mother? How deeply is it linked with the socio-cultural demands of tradition? Has it sprung from the bottom of my heart or from the expectations of the people around me? And what was more significant between these two: the child or my own self, or both as one unit?' She paused at last. I was overwhelmed by her thoughts.

It was mainly the adoption of a child that we could think of or talk about whenever we sat together to relax. She was terribly concerned about the acceptance of the adopted child by members of our family and the community around us. She would get impatient at times. One day, she came to me as something new had occurred to her and said, 'Let us go to Lonavala with our respective parents. We will sit with them and tell them about our intention and together we will arrive at a collective decision. They have always been concerned about us. Don't you think that they have wondered about our childlessness after nine years of married life? They will be relieved from their painful disappointment on account of our being childless if we take them along with us in finalizing the matter. Don't you agree to the idea?' Aneri ended with her forefinger raised in the air.

And we did exactly what Aneri had wished. Our parents, mine and hers, declared happily, 'Go ahead with your plan. We would like to see both of you happily engaged in the activities of the child.' After this,

Aneri used to walk on air. She smiled most of the time. 'I find my life is like a waterless cloud floating across the afternoon sky,' Aneri had lamented once, sobbing heavily with the pain of her childless condition. To see her overflow with joy was a sight very rare for me.

We visited many institutes involved in social work and discovered that if one institution insisted on our holding a certain religious faith in order to adopt a child; another considered us extremely unfortunate for being childless; and yet another one would force us to donate as much as possible, by way of compensation in lieu of adopting a child from them.

Our heart would melt when we looked at the conditions in which the children at these institutions lived. Small children suffering from diseases. Children holding dirty plastic plates in their hands for a *jalebi* and *ganthia* given by a donor. Children eager to be lifted up in the loving arms of visitors. Children wearing clothes made out of coarse material received from a donor. Children crying incessantly as if their life is no better than a prolonged moan. The fact that they were motherless was reflected in their tiny faces.

Aneri remained composed amidst these miserable children. She thought of their tender hearts and their tender age. Her mind meandered through the realm which went beyond all the social considerations and personal expectations or aspirations. She knew just one thing that she would be a mother soon.

'Shall we do one thing?' Aneri came to me, asking. A question like this used to be the first line of each poem that occupied an important place in our life in that time. And we did that. We adopted a child.

'Shall we do one thing?' Aneri repeated, sitting next to me. 'Shall we invite our friends and relatives to a party and welcome the child? Instead of their sulkily viewing our child or seeking a chance to ask questions, let us invite them to celebrate the arrival of the child in our life.'

The party was arranged and the child was named during the celebrations. People had come to the party with several questions lurking in their mind. But they did not think it right to ask questions keeping in mind how joyous we both seemed.

Aneri would forget everything happening around her whenever she was with Jasud. *Jasud* was the name chosen by Aneri; it meant 'the hibiscus blossom'.

'Shall I tell you something?' She asked, charged by the colour of hibiscus. She added, 'I feel as if a river starts flowing when I drop just a handful of water, a hill emerges when I drop just a stone, a forest comes into existence when I sow just a seed in the earth. I feel empowered to the fullest.'

'Look, he is smiling. And isn't he looking at you? Oh, he is turning on his sides!,' said Aneri, overpowered as she was with the new experiences involved in bringing up a child. Each and every moment with Jasud was one of rare wonder, enlivening and invigorating her.

'I am getting younger while Jasud is getting older', she smiled. She ran around with Jasud in the house, playing hide-and-seek or other games with him.

Jasud held on to a broken toy-car, the wheel of a broken truck, a winking cat, a galloping horse which he put in Aneri's handbag, the one she took to the university where she taught. Aneri was thrilled with the interfusion of the codes of both their lives—Jasud and herself—shaping within her. 'You know what happened today', was the starting point of the stories Aneri wanted to narrate to me, which were always about the countless charms of Jasud.

Once, our doctor asked Jasud, 'What would you like to be? A teacher, a lawyer or a doctor?' Jasud promptly replied, 'I want to be a "W." 'He is learning the English alphabet. He finds the letter "W" very fascinating,' Aneri explained.

One day Jasud came to the kitchen, opened one of the cupboards, took out jars, opened their lids, and poured sugar, tea and rice on the floor. 'What are you doing?,' Aneri asked angrily. 'I am angry. I am very angry because I am hungry,' he replied at once. Aneri realized that he had adopted the role of an adult in order to express his need, reinforcing his existence, which he felt was being ignored, temporarily. Aneri grew increasingly more perceptive and insightful regarding Jasud's behaviour.

Jasud was eager to be taken out one day. I said: 'Are you ready to go?' He promptly replied,

Oh, yes, yes, my dear Daddy
I'll give you the key of the car, Daddy
I'll help you wear your shoes, Daddy
Let's leave the house quietly, Daddy
Before Ma shouts to me, Daddy
'Finish your home work
Before you leave,' Daddy
Are you ready
Oh, yes, yes my dear Daddy!

Aneri overheard the rhyme Jasud had just composed, and yelled at him: 'Jasud, where are you going? Finish your homework first.' After saying this, she could not stop laughing aloud. Turning around, I looked at both of them. They were clinging to each other and Aneri was hugging him. This was the outcome of all sorts of rhymes Aneri came out with spontaneously while playing with Jasud.

Jasud developed a firm grip over our way of looking at things just as we developed an understanding about the fantastic manifestations of his primordial energy.

Aneri wrote a letter to Jasud when she was abroad doing research in Canada,

> I remember you
> Each gray day each wet day each snow-white day
> Whether it is Friday or Saturday or Sunday
> Whether it is the snowy glimmer of the trees
> Or the snowy dreamy hills
> What difference does it make
> To me or to Vancouver
> Sleeping in the lap of snow
> Without you!

Immediately on reading this Jasud sat down to write a letter to Aneri:

> Here goes my classic Mum
> Who knows how to solve every sum.
>
> Here goes my classic Mum
> Who cooks the food which makes me yum yum.
>
> Here goes my classic Mum
> Whose nose in the snow looks like a plum.

This is how maternal love, care and concern were intermingled with the child's response to the adult world, displaying both naivety and spontaneity.

'We have to pinch ourselves to remember that Jasud is our adopted child,' Aneri exclaimed happily one day. The glowing colour of hibiscus radiating in her existence kept Aneri constantly ignited.

The Mother Who Wasn't: Someone Who Should've been Born is Gone[1]

❧❧

Anwesha Arya

Is motherhood realized only when a child is actually born? What about the experience of conception? And if someone caught in a situation was unable to go through with a pregnancy, not because she didn't want to, but because she couldn't, does that count as motherhood?

Motherhood is an experience as varied as the women who experience it. The many essays and stories collected here reflect this. But what of the mother who wasn't, who couldn't be? In a volume on motherhood the experience of the mother who wasn't, is, I believe, as valid as the experience of the mother who was. Carrying a child for a few days is as intense an emotion as carrying a child to full-term. Or is it? I am not certain any one individual can conclusively rule on this. This piece is about the 'other', the un-mother—the mother who wasn't.

What I present here is a slice of my own mind. Processes, I developed in the darkness of my room, to torture and confuse myself. Intricate mental discussions I often return to, without a solution or closure after a dozen years or more.

Most women I know have experienced abortion at some point. Either by compulsion, either personally or they supported a friend or family member through the hushed back corridor of an unhygienic clinic. Yet, we do not talk about it openly and rarely among ourselves if we are in a group of three or more. Why do we consider abortion unspeakable? Is it really shameful? Or is it brave to elect the termination of a pregnancy not because the foetus cannot develop, but because you prefer it did not. Every secretive instinct rears itself and women cower into themselves protecting their non-existent bellies. So secretive that it is rarely brought up comfortably in one's own mind or memory. One of the terrifying outcomes of these repressed emotions is self-hatred. Women throw themselves continually into the metaphoric fire, judging themselves more harshly than would a jury comprising of one's enemies.

As a result, any support system is non-existent. Friends who may share their painful experiences tend to speak in the third person, if at all, or even construct an alternate identity for themselves.

'I *know* someone to whom it happened, but I never went through it myself.'

As if pain is dulled by proxy. So I won't. What if I write this piece in first person, as if it were my own story? It might even turn out to be more engaging.

I was seventeen, a young seventeen. It was 1989. We were both just out of school, and I was convinced I had found the love of my life. I had never been happier. For eight months, we experimented with ourselves. Getting to know our bodies and each other's, it was exhilarating. We hid—we found places where no one would be. We planned. We sneaked around giggling in the dark. And then it happened. I missed a period. My body usually went like well-greased machinery. Since the age of eleven, every 28 days I bled like a ripe plum. I was late by a few days. Three, I think.

I knew. I was pregnant.

Suddenly the reality of being an adult didn't seem exciting. For a week I waited. I pressed my fist into my stomach and took too many hot baths. I tried to make myself bleed. I felt trapped and stupid. I had just entered junior college; it was no time for a baby. Then I thought if I didn't think about it, perhaps it would go away. My head seemed too small to hold my brain. Nothing seemed normal anymore; I couldn't laugh with my friends as easily at the silliest jokes. When he came to hold me I didn't feel like cuddling him anymore. I wanted to be left alone. No one noticed the difference. I was writing angry poems making terrible rhymes. I pretended I was not me. I laughed louder, trying hard to fool myself. Should I tell him? He would hate me. It was my responsibility. I had to tackle it. What if I did not tell him, might be? Maybe it was not real. Maybe, I was imagining it. I was growing up still—my body changing fast. After all it was the first time I had missed a period.

Then I felt this rooted thing inside me, something that was growing. I sensed definite changes in my body—and new things happening. I couldn't pretend. So I decided to confide in my sister-in-law. She was only a few years older and had advised me about taking the necessary precautions with my body. She knew that my boyfriend and I didn't just hold hands. In fact, she used to tease me that I would never know if any boy loved me for me or for my body. (I had, then, the hourglass figure I crave today.) She would understand, I hoped.

I will never forget that evening. I waited for her to be alone in my brother's bedroom. My father was out for dinner. I went into the room, my head hanging as if my hair was weighed down by a pair of 5 kilo hair clips. My neck hurt so much I didn't look her in the eye. I sat down on the floor at the foot of their cane double bed. She was reading something intently. I held my face in my hands and waited for her to notice me. 'Oh no,' I remember her voice as if it was this morning. I couldn't identify any particular emotion, but disappointment and irritation were there. My head hung lower.

She drove me to the gynaecologist the next morning. It was cloudy and dark all along the horizon and I felt the clouds looming inside. Normally, I love the onset of the monsoon but that day I felt as if I was going to the dentist. The clouding grey and white of the sea did nothing to cheer me up. I didn't need any test to tell me what my body was saying. My breasts were heavier and slightly sore. My waist didn't feel the same. My lower back had coiled itself like an angry snake about to strike. I hated my body for cheating me. I hated myself. The feeling in my tummy was stronger and I wanted to change my life.

So many things rushed through my head as we sat there in the tiny waiting room. The roses on the receptionist's desk were dead. There was a strong smell of disinfectant and dampness, the walls were covered with posters of smiling babies. I wondered, why none of the babies were Indian, or girls? Gigantic blue eyes and blond dimpled boys stared down at me;

unexpectedly, I wanted to throw-up. The face of a round-eyed, chubby-cheeked child giggled aloud from the wall. I was terrified.

The only other lady waiting was alone. Her face was streaked with tears. Her bright red bangles matched the *sari* she was wearing and the dead flowers on the desk, at her elbow. Her belly could barely be hidden. She went in before us. The cubicle door slid shut, but through the wide cracks around the plywood we could hear their voices clearly.

'Why have you come now? I told you five months is just not possible.'

'But he left me ... I ....' Then was silence. She must have started to cry quietly. My sister-in-law leafed through the pages of the *Filmfare* magazine loudly.

'But I thought you were getting married?' The gynaecologist said in a steely tone.

'That's what he said ... then he started sleeping with my sister. She is older than me. She has the loop so she cannot get ....' The woman was snivelling.

'Oh God ...' the doctor sounded more annoyed than sympathetic, like this wasn't new to her. 'Now the best thing is to have this child and then give it up ... how old are you?'

'Nine ... no twenty. How can I do that? I don't want this child ... I don't want him.'

'You *should* have thought of that before. Now take this, try and stay calm. Where are they now ....' She sounded just like our school head teacher when someone had been caught cheating at an exam.

'He's taken her to Pune to meet his family. He said it is not his child I am carrying. He blames my neighbour ....' Her sniffing seemed infectious. I rubbed my nose and my sister-in-law shot me an arched eyebrow. My head was reeling. I avoided the grinning babies. What if he left me?

The door slid open and I could see inside. My feet and calves had turned to clay. Inside the doctor's cabin everything was flooded in a pale blue light. The walls, the examination room curtain, the sheet on the narrow leather bed, even the writing paper on her desk was a yucky, almost-white shade of blue. She smiled at my sister-in-law. 'Everything all right now?'

'Yes ... I'm fine. My *friend* is not.'

I wondered why she pretended I was her friend.

I didn't like the doctor's face. She looked like she hadn't eaten for days, her expression, I mean. She was quite fat otherwise. Three thick hairs protruded from her pimpled chin as she bent her face to examine me. I felt dirty. A darkened bit of skin made a mole under her left eye and her face was blotchy. She reminded me of the witch from the Snow White cartoon. I didn't really want her to touch me. Her eyes lit up as she dripped my urine from a little tube onto a test pack.

'Yes, you are carrying.' Her face looked more terrifying when she smiled.

'What do you want to do?,' my sister-in-law asked. It wasn't really a question.

'I want to talk to him and ... and till when can I decide?'

'We can't do anything after the 12th week.' The gynaecologist grinned again. I thought of our butcher. He grinned exactly like that when I asked him for the waste meat pieces for our dogs. I really didn't like her.

'We'll do a D&C ...,' and suddenly, seeing my bewildered expression, she replied slowly as if she had just realized my age. She looked at my sister-in-law with rising brows,

'Dilation and cutterage ... '

'You'll cut my ...' I couldn't stop myself. She nodded knowingly, now she knew my age. 'We go through your vagina, dear .... ' Who or what was she calling 'dear'? I wanted to go home and stand under the shower.

When I got home I called him. He was very calm, 'You *know* if we were older ... I don't want you to go through ... ' I understood immediately. He wanted me to make up my mind, but he thought we were too young. And we were.

So I chose.

The next five weeks I wanted to cry everyday. Why wasn't I twenty-one? We could have married. Why wasn't I born somewhere else? I could have had my baby and written a novel all together. We were studying Sylvia Plath's poetry at college and a horrible picture of the stench of baby puke and crap floated before me. Plath's words were acid, burning little holes into my imaginary world of him, and our baby and me. That night I called him when everyone had gone to sleep and cried a little. 'What if I go away to Ooty and have the child? Then we can adopt it back when we're older and married?' Before he answered I knew how idiotic it was.

Like the growing root in my tummy I felt trapped.

The next week he went to Goa with his friends. I was hurt. I couldn't go anywhere. Girls in those days were not allowed to travel by themselves. I did not normally lie and I hated hiding so I could not sneak off with him. I had never hated being a girl so much. So little freedom and then when you had it, it explodes in your face like a badly-made fire cracker. I finally spoke to my mother. My sister-in-law would be on tour with her play when the D&C was scheduled. I needed someone there. I did not want to tell my mother. Her reaction was amazing, like I was not her child but someone who needed support. After all she was a feminist social worker, I was glad she didn't get emotional. I was feeling enough emotion for every wounded woman in the world.

He called me from Goa, and I could make out in the tone of his voice that he had been crying. He wanted to be older, he said quietly. He wanted to be able to have this baby he said. We both loved each other and wanted a home together. The inevitability of things began to cloud my mind.

In class, on the Monday before the final appointment, I got a shock. We were handed out photocopies of a poem by one of Sylvia Plath's contemporaries, Anne Sexton. We had to analyse it critically:

The Abortion

Somebody who should've been born is gone.

Just as the earth puckered its mouth,
each bud puffing out of its knot,
I changed my shoes, and then drove south.

Up past the Blue Mountains, where,
Pennsylvania humps on endlessly,
wearing, like a crayoned cat, its green hair.

its roads sunken in like a gray washboard;
where, in truth, the ground cracks evilly,
a dark socket from which the coal has poured,

Somebody who should've been born is gone.

the grass as bristly and stout as chives,
and me wondering how anything fragile survives;

up in Pennsylvania, I met a little man,
not Rumplestiltskin, at all at all ...
he took the fullness that love began.

Returning north, even the sky grew thin
like a high window looking nowhere.
The road was as flat as a sheet of tin.

Somebody who should have been born is gone.

Yes, woman, such logic will lead
To loss without death. Or say what you meant,
you coward ... this baby that I bleed.[2]

My mouth filled slowly with bitter bile. I swallowed it and glanced around the classroom. Had anyone noticed my quavering fingers or restless feet? Everyone seemed immersed in the problem of analysis. I did not need to think for an instant, I knew. I felt it. I understood. I stayed silent through the class, listening to every inane suggestion. Why the use of 'crayoned cat'? What significance did the sprouting chives hold? And the refrain? Was she guilty or relieved?

'She's confused ...' I wanted to scream.

I've always hated Mondays. The nurse who shaved me was younger than me. I suddenly felt clean, like a baby. Her hands felt soft as she wiped me down, and she smelled distinctly of Johnson's baby talcum powder. She smiled a lot but didn't speak till the other older nurse came in. They looked at me and held a muted conversation in Malayalam. He and *Ma* were waiting outside. The hospital gown felt rough against my dimpling skin. They couldn't find the control for the air conditioning. 'Doctor iz zimply too buzy today. You wait okay, don't move now ....' Her accent would have been funny if I was feeling anything at the time. The anesthesiologist was late. I waited in the green operating room alone. I hate anesthesiologists; they are so smug and superior. I felt his fat damp fingers probing my arm for a suitable place to fill the fluid. He was a short man, like Rumplestiltskin, I heard him chattering about what a slim figure I had with the doctor—in that half-conscious state of warm grey light I wanted to slap him. My brain wouldn't send the command to my hand and I suppose I passed out soon after. But, before the silent darkness my heavy head thudded the single line 'Some-one who should've been born ....'

It was a dreamless unconsciousness. I don't recall a single image. When I came round, his large face was resting against mine, heavy with the hurt in his eyes. We looked at each other silently. An emptiness that no words could fill, rapidly filled the small room. My mother came in with a cup of very sweet tea. She wasn't smiling. The two of us shared it. Sipping slowly, with me watching his large lips. I wanted to pretend I didn't want it, I should have acted the victim but I felt none of the pain I thought

I would. Besides I was dying for the milky tea. He said later he knew he could not share everything with me, but he wanted to. The gown was slightly stained with blood. The sight made me want to retch. He held me so close. I could feel the tiny hairs on the base of his neck tickling the side of my cheek. He had bought me a Tintin to read. I loved him. We would have other children I thought, watching his eyes watching me. The pain did come, later that night. It was not physical.

I bled for 10 days. I held the ache much longer. That blood was different. It was not mine. I wanted to take out my womb and bury it. I wanted it to rot.

Life's metaphors are excruciating when you recognize them. Several years later, after many relieved periods punching their way through my uterine muscles, it happened again. And still the time was wrong. We were still not ready for marriage. The bizarre thing was the timing.

My mother was suffering with a hormonal condition, a hysterectomy was advised. She was admitted into a maternity nursing home. This time I didn't tell her. She had made me promise never to put her through that again. I did not want to. It happened. The way it usually does. Sneaky thing, life—creeps up on you.

So, there we were—mother and daughter—me caring for her, preparing her for the possible loss of the symbol of motherhood—her womb. All the time I was aware that the following week I'd be terminating my own motherhood, again. That night *Ma* slept, to use a cliché, like a baby. I wonder why we say that. Babies are terrible sleepers, it is legendary. In fact, that night as I watched the fan move aimlessly, spreading no breeze, *Ma* snored peacefully and I wished I could plug my brain when a terrible shrieking broke out in the adjoining baby ward. Three abandoned babies had been born the previous day. *Ma* slept on. I leapt to my feet and followed the white capped nurse to the cot where the inhuman shriek came from. It was an ugly, shrivelled child. The skin bunched unnaturally around the tiny eyelids and chin. The mouth was wider than its face, it seemed. The nurse smiled at me as she lifted the tightly bound bundle. It looked very like an ancient Egyptian ready for the afterlife. The baby was still crying, 'You want to hold her ...' I held my arms out without a thought in my mind. As my hands touched the bundle of cotton, the shrieking was subdued, the eyes opened and I saw a cloudy colour, between deep blue and milky black. They couldn't focus, but I felt she was looking at me. I rocked her gently. No one had taught me that. The silence after the screaming was lovely. I was holding her like my arms were glued to the swathes around her. The nurse let me take her into our room. *Ma* was awake. She cooed at the baby.

That night I stayed up, cradling someone else's unwanted girl, while the one growing inside me didn't cry or move. I was a mother for a few hours, I think. The following night another of life's excruciating metaphors made itself known to me. I was staying at my grandmother's house. My cousins were in town for the summer holidays. We always had midnight feasts pretending to be characters from some Enid Blyton book. It was just what the proverbial doctor ordered. We snuck around the house looting the fridge of chocolate and condensed milk. I was just beginning to feel twelve again when the weird cries of one of the cats made us go to the office room. Cleo, one of the younger cats (my grandmother had around 38 cats then) was writhing in pain. Her pale marmalade body horribly arched. Half-sitting, half-lying, Cleo was bleeding all over my grandfather's precious leather-covered desk.

We watched her, and then with the instinct that had developed inside me, I asked my cousin to fetch a large mug of warm water and some towels or old cloth. Cleo meowed pitifully. I tried to pet her tummy. Her slim body convulsed with violent spasms. I was convinced she was dying in the process of giving birth. Suddenly, her body went taut and her eyes glazed like dull lozenges. I held her, caressing her chin. Just as my cousin brought in the water, Cleo pumped a half-formed kitten onto the deep green leather in a pool of almost black blood. I bathed her stomach and stroked it continually, she seemed to relax. Then again she convulsed, her pale-gold orange fur prickling under my fingers. Another little aborted foetus. My face and hands felt numb. I didn't understand what I was meant to learn from this experience. Why?

If my experience counts as a truncated version of motherhood, then I know I am not alone. Most women have experienced it. It is the other side of motherhood. The dark, barely-explored side. It has been expressed in poems and fiction, but we still won't talk about it. We pretend it wasn't us. We deny it because society does not make room for someone reaching out and saying, 'I went through it too'. Most often your own conscience judges you, 'murderer' or 'irresponsible'. I wanted to tell someone, someone may have wanted to tell me. Now I won't even talk to myself about it.

Since then, I have heard about a friend's cousin who had six abortions and can no longer conceive. There are stories about a well-loved actress who could not admit her affair with her married lover and was forced into 12-terminated pregnancies. She went on to have children quite late in her life. These stories were swapped as warnings, of the terrible things that could maim your reputation. Never was a woman who went through an aborted pregnancy to be empathized with. I don't understand. I cannot. Not only because I have been in that horrible green room, on a creaky spider-legged stretcher bed waiting to pluck out a part of myself. Waiting and listening, while my mind accused me of being a traitor, a murderer, a stony non-woman. But also because I had no argument. I felt all those things. I stood accused and guilty.

It strikes me as both fascinating and tragic that so deep and universal an experience cannot be more widely shared. I know I needed support. We both did, him and me. We gave it to each other, without talking about it. But this cloud-like taboo hangs over the feeling to this day. Its like the other face of suicide is abortion. The 'A' word, the unspeakable act. I imagine if there was to be a religious sentence like for suicides who were banned from receiving a proper burial, women who have abortions will remain perpetually outside solace. What then happens to aborted foetuses?

While researching this article on the Internet, I came across the website where Anne Sexton's poem is posted. *The Abortion* has 16 comments; it is outdone only by the poem exploring suicide. All the commentators seem to be women. Interestingly, being an American poet, the comments are posted by Americans who are almost all using the space to air their views about pro-life arguments and the evil practice of aborting a foetus. One heart-rending account, in badly spelled words, articulated her case in favour of going through a pregnancy arguing that it was your god-given duty to go through with a pregnancy. She had been raped; her own mother was a juvenile offender and locked in prison. And this girl argued the case for bringing into this world the most potent reminder of her trauma. I felt confused.

Today, with the explosion in technology, where perfect 3D imaging allows would-be parents to see the growing embryo in clear images, it becomes harder to argue pro-choice. These images are being exploited to convince would-be mothers to recognize their foetus as a person. In the UK, the plan is to use this new technology to discourage women smokers who continue their habit through pregnancies. In any case, the dilemmas relating to abortions are as unique as the cases themselves. The pros and cons on both sides are valid and endless. If we shared our thoughts, discussed the emotional upheavals and attempted to understand the nerve-endings of this issue we may come close to clearing the cobwebs. Young girls are still facing the same dilemmas faced by others decades ago, or even a couple of centuries ago. Mike Leigh's film *Vera Drake* has put a different twist to the argument, bringing a different aspect of this deeply disturbing issue to light: that of the abortionist.

It is easy to moralize about giving life or that all life is sacred. Fortunately, as an atheist I do not have the additional itch of religious morality. The easiest argument against aborting is that it is a selfish choice, convenient to erring adults, and that no one considers the rights of the foetus. What about victims of rape who become pregnant? Or a daughter carrying her father's child? What about a girl who is a child herself? A deep-seated lack of consciousness allows the confusion to continue and abound.

But is it sufficient to create life? What about sustaining it? Isn't nurturing a child as important? I am the product of a troubled marriage and yet, I valued the context of having a family, whatever shade it was. Besides, when I think of it, if I had gone ahead with my pregnancy and then given my child up for adoption how would I have felt? I could not have lived with the knowledge that a child somewhere had my imprint and that of my love, but didn't have the luxury of our affection. I chose to terminate my motherhood; both of us went against our initial instinct. We knew we wanted to have our baby, but we were too young. It is terribly hard to say this, but I think I made the right decision. At least I'd like to believe I did.

Others have other extenuating circumstances. Some do not. In India, today, abortion clinics are always fully booked. But the dazed young mothers who can't call themselves mothers, stumble homeward in darkness. Few of us can offer consolation. If we could, most of us would. Because most of us know the unlit path through that densely silent darkness, at least we can reach out and guide ourselves through it.

Someday, I'd like to be a mother. If my body gives up on me, then I'll hate myself again. But I will find a way out. I did not opt to write letters like one mother who wasn't. She famously addressed her trauma to her unborn child. I wrote a poem before I saw Sexton's. It was childish and half-formed, but it was the only way to express at the time. Soon after, I showed the poem to one of my brother's friend's girlfriends, who was a journalist. She nodded her head at me, 'You should write about experiences you know ... really *know*.' 'I do,' the words hovered on the tip of my tongue, but I didn't tell her or anyone else about the discomfort that kept me up most nights. My sister-in-law never asked me how I felt. Ignoring the event seemed the only way for everyone to deal with it. Did it work? I am not sure. I ignore it today; then I couldn't. I know and understand closure. But death, in whatever form, is incomprehensible. Religions have been developed around tackling these deep, difficult emotions in society. We are still no closer to explaining how best to deal with death. When my father died nine years ago, people with genuine concern for my welfare said serenely 'time heals all'. I don't agree. I wish they hadn't lied. I suppose they didn't mean to. The only thing that has happened is that the distance has dulled the immediacy of the loss. I missed the physical presence of my father, I still do. The loss feels no less. When I had my abortions the toughest part was dealing with the intangibles. How do you deal with an empty space that you didn't actually ever see as full? How could you miss holding a child you had never physically ever held?

Do I regret it? I'm not sure. It seemed the right thing to do at the time. I can't rationalize it. I don't want to. It didn't leave an empty ache or any identifiable emotion, or any clichéd storm of pain. I don't blame anyone, only the timing.

We're married now. We have not since revisited that small box-like room, where we forged a bond. It remains unspeakable. Sometime ago, one of my dearest friends lost her baby 20 minutes before she could deliver. I was away from Bombay when it happened but I felt the wrench, just as if something had been torn from me. Perhaps I should have written telling her. I haven't. Maybe I could have said I have some vantage point from which to understand her terrible helplessness in the face of life. We could've shared something deeper if I had reached out, something no one can really explain. But I chose not to. I have not spoken about these experiences or emotions before. Not to friends and not even with my husband, who shares the knowledge of this past in his own silent way. It cannot be erased, it cannot be denied. But why can't it be shared?

Once I had thought holding a baby would be impossible. Today, I look into eyes that still haven't learnt to focus and I wonder. I imagine, but can I ever know what might have been? It is impossible to argue about choices, and right and wrong. I believe that its crucial to take responsibility for a life you take part in creating. It is important to bring up, not just give birth. We will have children when we can. I hope.

And yet, sometimes when I'm alone on a bus, in a crowd of silent commuters, those words sway into my mind like a song, 'Somebody who should've been born is gone.'

I know.

Afterword

The resonance of the title, the very content of this essay has returned to haunt me it seems. Shortly after I completed this piece last year, I conceived. It was an unexpected and uphill pregnancy, but I was delirious with the timing. We both were. Finally. We had just bought our first home, we got confirmation of the pregnancy and the keys to our house the same day. It was *Diwali*. Nothing could be more auspicious, even to an atheist.

On 7 May 2006 our daughter was born. A full head of gorgeous curls, just above eight pounds, and almost two feet tall. Perfect hands, and feet sculpted to dance. But she never opened her eyes. I have been robbed of my chance to gaze into their cloudiness, and I still wonder about being a mother.

Now I hear the words, repeating themselves rhythmically:
'someone who should've been born
is gone ...'
'someone who should've been born
is gone ...'

and imagine her tiny feet, thump, to their beat.

Notes

1. This line is from Anne Sexton's poem *The Abortion*.
2. Anne Sexton, *The Abortion*, available online at http://vmlinux.org/ilse/lit/sexton.htm

Glossary

aai (Marathi):	mother
ab samajh main ayaa bachchu (Hindi):	now do you understand, mischievous child
addas (Bengali):	lively chatting sessions in Bengal
akka (Tamil/Telegu):	older sister
amla (Hindi):	phyllanthus emblica
amma:	mother
amra (Hindi):	sour green berries with small hard seeds
anganwadi (Hindi):	creche
annas:	Indian currency, one-sixteenth of a Rupee (now discontinued)
anturghar (Bengali):	the inner birthing place for women in Bengal
aparajita (Bengali):	the unvanquished, the indefatigable
apro (Gujarati):	ours/belonging to our community
arangetram (Tamil):	first public dance (specifically Bharatnatyam) performance
attha (Telegu):	father's sister
avakkai:	big, raw mangoes cut into pieces and pickled in the Andhra style
ayahs (Hindi):	maids who look after children
baanjh (Hindi):	barren
baba (Bengali):	father
badan (Hindi/Bengali):	visage
bai (Hindi/Marathi):	maidservant/midwife
baidya/vaidya:	in the Bengali Hindu caste hierarchy the Baidyas are considered a notch below the Brahmins and higher than Kayasthas. Intercaste marriages even within the same community were taboo and considered to be a transgression of social mores
baper bari:	colloquial Bengali word used to describe one's natal home

bhabi (Hindi):	brother's wife
bhadralok:	bengali for middle-class, also connotes respectability
bhai (Hindi):	brother
bhajan (Hindi):	devotional songs
bhakti:	devotion
bhelpuri:	mixture of crisp savouries
bhelwala:	person who sells bhelpuri
bhindi:	lady's finger
bhoj (Bengali):	banquet
bijoya-dashmi:	the tenth day of Durga Puja, when the image of the Goddess is immersed, thereby, marking the end of festivities
bindi:	decorative motif worn by Indian women on their forehead
bonti (Bengali):	sharp blade on a wooden base, used for cutting vegetables, fish, etc.
bori (Bengali):	savouries made of ground pulses, which are then sun-dried; used in curries
brahmras:	divine nectar
carnatik:	classical music of South India
chakkars (Hindi):	going around in circles
chapatis (Hindi):	hand-baked Indian bread
chappals (Hindi):	sandals or footwear
chhi! (Bengali):	shame
chhuara:	dried aril or mace added in cooking, for aroma and flavour
chiku:	a sweet fruit
chitpavan brahmins:	considered uppermost within the Brahmin hierarchy
chullah (Hindi):	a clay oven with coal as fuel
chutney:	Indian preserve
dahi-chuda (Bengali):	flattened rice and sugar, a breakfast delicacy
dal, bhat, sabji (Bengali):	pulses, rice, vegetables
dandia ras:	folk dance during the Dussera celebrations
dhanvantara (Sanskrit):	herbal oil, considered as a good tonic for hair growth/body massage during women's pregnancy/post-natal care
didi:	elder sister in Indian language
dil dhoondhta hai phir vahi fursat ke raat din (Hindi):	O, how the heart longs for those days of leisure
Diwali:	festival of lights

doddama (Tamil): older aunt/wife of father's elder brother

dookhi (Bengali): unfortunage, sad

dosai: fermented, lentil crepes; a South Indian delicacy

dyaneshwari: devotional couplets composed by the Saint Poet Dyaneshwar from Maharashtra

elaichi (Hindi): cardamom

eto (Bengali): food eaten by another/shared food.

Gandhian: followers of Mahatma Gandhi's philosophy

ganthia: salty savouries

gehne banwao, gehne tudwao: make and remake ornaments

gheraoed (Hindi): surrounded

gita pravachan: discourse by a scholar to elaborate and interpret the verses of the Bhagvad Gita—the composite philosophical and spiritual guide to purposeful action, attributed to Lord Krishna

goondas (Hindi): ruffians

guru: mentor

gyan (Hindi): lessons, wisdom

Holi: the festival of colours celebrated to mark the coming of spring

jagat janani (Bengali): universal mother

jaiphal (Hindi): nutmeg

jalebis (Hindi): crisp curly Indian sweets

jamai babu (Bengali): Brother-in-law/sister's husband

janani janma bhumishcha swargya dopi goriosee (Sanskrit): a Sanskrit line that means mother and motherland are greater than even heaven

jaroa (Bengali): studded

jutka (Kannada): horse-drawn cart

kaazi: muslim cleric

kajus: cashew nuts

kanji (Marathi): a drink made from rice

kanthas (Bengali): quilts made from old *sari*s

karela: bitter gourd

karta (Bengali): head of the household/patriarch

kathak dance: a particular dance form, popular in the Courts of Maharajas

khadi: hand woven cloths

khayal: an evolved art form of North Indian Classical Music

Khichdi-choka
  (Bengali): kedgeree cooked with spicy mashed potato
khurima: wife of father's younger brother
kirtana: devotional music
kudrum: wild shrub of the hibiscus family bearing fruits that have red petals over oval green seeds. The petals are sour in taste and used for making pickles
kul: a kind of wild plum that grows in abundance throughout India
lathi-charged: beating with a stick
ma: mother
machaan (Hindi): treetop perch built for keeping vigil. The word has been famously used in the hunting stories of Jim Corbett
madur (Bengali): straw mat
mahila samaj (Hindi): women's organization
mai (Marathi): mother
mali (Hindi): gardener
malpua-choley
  (Bengali): a syrupy sweet condiment made during the festival of Holi, alongwith a spicy dish of chick peas
mama: maternal uncle, mother's brother
mamabari (Bengali): the home of the mother's brother—signifies, a place of joy
mangalagaur: an auspicious occasion
mashima: mother's sister
mathu-banoo: head scarf
matri bhakti: devotee of mother
matri devi: formal address for the mother
matri rin: debt owed to one's mother
mausam: season
morcha (Hindi): road-side demonstrations
mung dal (Hindi): yellow lentil
namaste (Hindi): a respectful gesture with folded hands used for greeting people
nana (Hindi): maternal grandfather
nani (Hindi): maternal grandmother
narialpani (Hindi): coconut water
neelibhringadi
  (Sanskrit): a cooling hair oil made of indigenous herbs
niramish (Bengali): vegetarian
pappad: salty savoury
patibrata
  (Hindi/Bengali): devoted wife

paush-sankranti
  (Bengali):   or Makar Sankranti, the 14th of January, cele-
                            brated as a harvest festival in different parts of
                            India
pipal: bo tree
pishima (Bengali):   father's sister
pital-handi: copper cooking pan
puja: worship
puja mandir: place of worship
Raga Neelambari: a musical
rangolis: floor decorations
rasam: soup of lentils, south Indian style
rashtriya mela: was a patriotic music squad
rassogollas: round Bengali sweets made of cottage cheese
rickshawalla: auto driver
sada satyabadi
  (Bengali):   always truthful
sahib or saheb: the boss
saraswati puja: puja celebrated in honour of the Goddess
                            Saraswati
saral (Bengali):   simpleton
sarbamatyantam
  garhitam (Sanskrit): too much of anything is bad
sasurbari (Bengali):   the in-laws home
sati: the practice of burning widows alive on the funeral
                            pyre of their husbands. Followed in 18th century
                            Bengal
satranchi (Bengali):   mat
savati (Telegu):   step mother, half siblings
shakto: a religious cult where female energy was deified
                            and worshipped. Founded by Maha Paribajyak
                            Acharya through his treatise 'Kamyo Jantradhar'
                            in 1375 A.D. which institutionalized the cult as a
                            religion. In 1425 Sarbananda spread the message
shaman: death
shastras: religious texts
shlokas: sanskrit verses
shravan: spring
sindhi: community hailing from Sindhu
singhara, kachuri,
  dalpuri (Bengali):   wheat based delicacies with a variety of stuffing
                            and deep fried
sondesh (Bengali):   soft white sweet, famous in Bengal and made with
                            cottage cheese

tabla:	popular Indian percussion instrument used as an accompaniment in classical performances
tanam:	in the creative elaboration of Carnatic music, a raga is elaborated in *alapanai* followed by *tanam*, which is a manipulation of the three syllabus *aa, nam, tham* and it ends with a *pallavi*, a lyric set in complicated rhythmic patterns
tarkari (Bengali):	cooked vegetables
tehsil:	a district
thakurma (Bengali):	father's mother
tilek:	a colloquial expression that means a moment
tuka:	the pet name of Saint Tukaram
vadam:	south Indian puffed rice savoury
vaishnava:	was founded by Jamunacharya and spread by Ramanuj Acharya (1116–1137 A.D.). This cult worshipped Laxmi, the goddess of wealth and her consort Lord Vishnu. Vaishanavism as propounded by Sri Chaitanya (1486–1533) preached the message of love and forgiveness and was a counter to the caste system prevailing in Bengal. Born in Nabadweep (Nadia district, W. Bengal) as Nemai he was affectionately referred to as 'Nader Nemai' (Nemai of Nadia)
vanvas:	exile
vatsavitri:	religious ceremony observed by married Hindu women
veshti:	attire worn by men in South India
vidyan (Bengali):	wise, educated
zafran (Hindi):	saffron

About the
Editor and Contributors

The Editor

Rinki Bhattacharya is Chairperson of the Bimal Roy Memorial Committee. She is also a well-known journalist and documentary film-maker based in Mumbai. Her documentary, *Char Diwari*, on domestic violence has received international acclaim. She made a five-minute audio-visual capsule, *Janani*—based on the same theme as this book. Ms Bhattacharya has also worked as a volunteer at Nari Kendra in Mumbai and started, in 1987, a crisis hotline called Help. Her publications include *Bengal Spices* (2005), *Behind Closed Doors: Domestic Violence in India* (2004), *Indelible Imprints—Daughters Write on Fathers* (1999), *Uncertain Liaisions: Sex, Strife & Togetherness in Urban India* (1996), *Bimal Roy—A Man of Silence* (1994), *Cuisine Creations from Bengal* (1993), monograph on the film-maker Bimal Roy, monograph on film-star Ashok Kumar, genres of Indian Cinema—Les star Du Indian Cinema.

Contributors

Anwesha Arya is currently enrolled for her Ph.D. in the Department of the Study of Religions, School of Oriental and African Studies (SOAS), University of London. She is researching the shift from bride-price practices to dowry in India and dowry-related murders. Ms Arya has previously been published in *Behind Closed Doors: Domestic Violence in India* (edited by Rinki Bhattacharya, 2004) and *A Flash of Red* (2005).

Jasodhara Bagchi is Chairperson of the West Bengal State Women's Commission. Educated at Presidency College, Kolkata, Somerville College, Oxford, and New Hall, Cambridge, a large part of her working life was spent at Jadavpur University, where she was Professor of English. In 1988, Professor Bagchi became the Founder-Director of the School of Women's Studies at Jadavpur University, in which capacity she led the activities of the centre until her retirement in 1997. She initiated and spearheaded the pioneering Bengali Women Writers Reprint Series edited by the School of Women's Studies, Jadavpur University, and is also one of the founder-members of the feminist organization, Sachetana, in Kolkata. Among Professor Bagchi's numerous authored, edited and co-edited volumes are *The Changing Status of Women in West Bengal, 1970–2000: The Challenge Ahead* (2005), *The Trauma and the Triumph: Gender and Partition in India* (2003) and *Thinking Social Science in India: Essays in Honour of Alice Thorner* (2002).

Neela Bhagwat is a renowned *Khayal* singer. Trained in the pristine purity of the Gwalior Gharana, Neela has also been exposed to the Indian progressive movement. Her participation in the feminist activities and the struggle for socio-cultural transformation, has enhanced her stature as an artiste. Her interpretations of Kabir, Meerabai, Tukaram, Chokhamela and Mahatma Phule through music constitute a major milestone. Her own compositions expressing contemporary concerns like feminism and communal harmony, have won her a wide acclaim.

Maitreyi Chatterji is a prominent human rights & women's rights activist. With Shoma Marik, she co-edited a report on atrocities committed on women in the 2002 riots in Gujarat under the caption, *Garbhaghati Gujrat*. Ms Chatterji has contributed articles to *Whose News? The Media and Women's Issues* (edited by Ammu Joseph and Kalpana Sharma, 2006) and *Faces of the Feminine in Ancient, Medieval, and Modern India* (edited by Mandakranta Bose, 2000).

Kamala Das (Madhavikutty), is one of the most prolific writers of her generation. Her first short story collection, *Mathilukal* (Walls), was published in 1955. *Pathu Kathakal* (Secret Stories) followed in 1958 and *Narichirukal Parakkumpol* (When Little Bats Fly) in 1960. Kamala Das' first and best collection of poems in English, *Summer in Calcutta* (1965), was followed by *The Descendants* (1967) and *The Old Playhouse* (1973). A heart attack in the early 1970s did not stop her from contesting the parliamentary elections as an independent candidate from Trivandrum in 1984. Though she lost, she got extremely good press coverage for her campaign, during which she spoke out against the hypocrisy and corruption in public life. She was awarded the Chimanlal Award for fearless journalism in 1986.

Shashi Deshpande is a distinguished novelist and short story writer. She has received awards for three of her novels, including the Sahitya Akademi award for *That Long Silence* (1988). Ms Deshpande's novels and short stories have been translated into many Indian and European languages. Her recent publications include *Writing from the Margin and Other Essays* (2003) and *Moving On* (2004).

Nabaneeta Dev Sen is a scholar of international repute. She has recently retired as Professor of Comparative literature at Jadavpur University, Calcutta. Professor Sen was recently nominated as the J.P. Naik Distinguished Fellow at the Centre for Women's Development Studies, New Delhi, 2003–05. She has received many National Awards, including the Lifetime Achievement Award from the State Literary Academy (Bangla Akademi), the Central Literary Academy Award (Sahitya Akademi) and the President's Award, Padmashri. Nabaneeta Dev Sen has published more than 60 books in Bengali—novels, short stories, poetry, plays, literary criticism, personal essays, travelogues, translations and memoirs and has contributed to several genres of children's literature as well. Her works have been translated into many languages in India and abroad.

Deepa Gahlot is a well-known journalist, critic, columnist and screenwriter. She started her career with *The Times of India*, before joining *Filmfare*, screenwriter and went on to become the Editor of *Sunday Mid Day* and *Cinema in India*. Ms Gahlot received the National Award for Best Film Criticism in 1998. Her recent publications include *The Prithwiwallahs* (with Shashi Kapoor, 2004).

Jyotsna Kamal is an electrical engineer by profession. She taught in IIT (Bombay), and was Principal, College of Engineering, Ponda, Goa. Professor Kamal has been very radical in her approach to politics and was an activist in the Communist Party of India (ML). Her book in Marathi, *Kale Pani*, is a translation of the biography of Marium Makeba and has been widely appreciated.

C.S. Lakshmi is currently the Director of SPARROW (Sound and Picture Archives for Research on Women). A renowned Tamil writer who writes in the pesudonym *Ambai*, C.S. Lakshmi has been a researcher in Women's Studies for the past 30 years. She was one of the three writers in the writers' delegation sent by Katha, New Delhi, to University of Texas at Austin, University of Chicago; University of Wisconsin at Madison, USA; School of Oriental and African Studies (SOAS), London; and Nehru Centre, London, to discuss literature, translation and culture. She was also Rockefeller Scholar-in-Residence, Institute for Culture and Consciousness in South Asia, University of Chicago, in 1992 and was awarded the Ford Foundation Fellowship from 1981–84. C.S. Lakshmi's recent publications include *Seven Seas and Seven Mountains: The Singer and the Song* (2000) and *An Illustrated Social History of Women in Tamil Nadu* (forthcoming).

Tutun Mukherjee is Professor and Head of the Centre for Comparative Literature, University of Hyderabad. Her current research interests are translation, women's writing, theatre and film studies. She has published widely in the above subjects.

Dhiruben Patel, a staunch Gandhian, has received several awards including the Gujarat Sahitya Akademi and the Sahitya Natak Akademi Award. Amongst the 50 odd books published are novels, novelettes, radio plays, collection of poems, and screenplays for children's films.

Urmila Pawar is one of the leading contemporary Dalit writers. Her published books include *Sahavan Bot, Udan, Amhihi Itihas Ghadavala, Chouthi Bhint, Mauritius Ek Pravas*, amongst others. Urmila Pawar has been honoured with the Sahitya Sanskruti Mandal Maharashtra Rajya Puraskar (1989), Asmitadarsh Puraskar (1989), Shakuntala Nene Puraskar (1992) and many others.

Nita Ramaiya has to her credit four books of poetry, two books of poetry for children, two books of stories for children, four books of Gujarati translations of Canadian literary texts, amongst others. Five of her books have received the highest literary awards from the Gujarat Sahitya Akademi and Gujarati Sahitya Parishad.

Pratibha Ranade has translated many books in Marathi. Prominent amongst them are, *Lamache Rahasya* (1973) and *Band Darwaza* (a Marathi translation of Amrita Pritam's novel by the same name, 1974). She has been awarded the Ford Foundation Research Grant and has received Best Book Awards for *Afghan Diary* and *Stri Prashnanchi Charcha*.

Maithili Rao is a freelance film critic and writer based in Bombay. A regular contributor to the London-based *South Asian Cinema* and *Frontline*, Ms Rao is also a columnist on current cinema for *Man's World*. She previously wrote a column on Images of Women for *Eves' Weekly* and has contributed chapters to *Britannica Encyclopaedia Volume on Hindi Cinema*, *Bollywood* (Dakini Publication), *Frames of Mind* (ICCR) and *Rasa*.

Bharati Ray taught History at Calcutta University and was the Pro-Vice Chancellor from 1988 to 1995. She was the Founder Director of the Women's Studies Research Centre, Calcutta University, and was Member, Rajya Sabha, from 1996 to 2002. Her books include *Early Feminists of Colonial India: Sarala Devi Chaudhurani and Rokeya Sakhawat Hossain* (2002), *From Independcence Towards Freedom: Indian Women Since 1947* (jointly edited with Aparna Basu, 1999).

Rekha Rodwittiya is a practicing artist who currently lives and works in Baroda along with her partner Surendran Nair. An alumni of the Faculty of Fine Arts, Baroda and the Royal College of Art, London, she is also an independent curator, writer, teacher and counsellor. Rekha Rodwittiya's works are exhibited in numerous private and public collections in India and abroad. She is a prolific painter and has travelled extensively to work on residency programmes and site-specific world art projects. Staunchly feminist, women's issues and gender politics are the areas of enquiry that remain pivotal within her work till date.

Mallika Sarabhai is a renowned Kuchipudi and Bharatnatyam dancer and Human Rights activist. She received her Doctorate from the Indian Institute of Management, Ahmedabad. Dr Sarabhai played the role of Draupadi in Peter Brook's *Mahabharata* and was awarded the Palme d' Or for Best Soloist Artist. She runs her dance academy, Darpana, in Ahmedabad.

Roshan G. Shahani had been a teacher of English literature for 38 years at Jai Hind College from where she retired as Head of the English Department. She is editor of *Beam* (Bombay English Association Magazine) and Trustee of SPARROW (Sound and Picture Archives for Research on Women). Her publications include *The Canadian Family in Fiction* and memoirs of her mother, *Allan, Her Infinite Variety* (published by SPARROW).